Praise for *Redemption*

"I'm a Martin Luther King Jr. devotee. When I was a boy growing up in the South in his wake, this Southern black man of towering intellect, soaring oratory, and piercing moral clarity was to me a beacon in the darkness, a template for a life lived with purpose. I still can't get enough of reading about him. So I recommend *Redemption*, by Joseph Rosenbloom. The granular detail of this slender volume is immersive, humanizing, and demystifying."

—CHARLES BLOW, *The New York Times*

"In this gripping account of the King assassination, Joseph Rosenbloom does more than recover the story of the hours leading up to that fateful shot at the Lorraine Motel in Memphis, April 1968. Writing with the urgency of a journalist's pen, Rosenbloom melts time away to redeem the fully human struggle of a man, a leader, under enormous pressure, risking his reputation and his life, trying to answer the question, Where do we go from here? The result is not only an absorbing narrative of what happened; it offers readers a chance to reflect on what might have been."

—HENRY LOUIS GATES JR.,
Alphonse Fletcher University Professor,
Harvard University

"A compelling and meticulously researched account by investigative journalist Joseph Rosenbloom, *Redemption* casts Martin Luther King Jr.'s last thirty-one hours into bold relief. With artful story-telling, the narrative draws the reader intimately into King's life and courageous moments at a time of grave danger to himself and the civil rights movement, constantly rewinding to provide crucial context. King's initial struggle to bolster striking sanitation workers in Memphis becomes a piece of the larger, transcendent story that *Redemption* vividly explores, one that still resonates powerfully today. It is the story of King's urgent crusade to end poverty in America."

—MICHAEL K. HONEY, author of *Going Down Jericho Road:
The Memphis Strike, Martin Luther King's Last Campaign*

"In this crisply wrought story, in this absolute thriller, I read courage like never before. Joseph Rosenbloom walks us through an American tragedy, a righteous American tragedy of a Martin Luther King Jr. unstinting in his final movement against poverty and racism. King comes to life in death—a courage ever so inspiring."

—IBRAM X. KENDI, author of *Stamped from the Beginning:
The Definitive History of Racist Ideas in America*

"Martin Luther King Jr. has remained a towering figure through so many decades, during which his dream has gone unfulfilled, that any account of his death at thirty-nine by an assassin's bullet outside a Memphis hotel still shocks, still feels freshly tragic. Yet Joseph Rosenbloom's *Redemption* is like no other. He tells the suspenseful story of King's last days in remarkable detail, illuminating King's increasing radicalism and intensifying purpose in a narrative that takes in both the worst and the best of human possibility."

—MEGAN MARSHALL, Pulitzer Prize–winning author of *Margaret Fuller: A New American Life* and *Elizabeth Bishop: A Miracle for Breakfast*

"*Redemption* is a rare, intimate account of Martin Luther King Jr.'s last stand. It is a story of courage and tragedy, a story of a man guided by deep religious faith in his quest to end poverty. More powerfully than any other, the book tells of his sacrifice for a cause that is as critically vital today to our nation's democracy and security as it was when he dedicated himself to it fifty years ago."

—JAMES MEREDITH, veteran civil rights activist and desegregation pioneer as the first to integrate the University of Mississippi

"Rosenbloom commits an extraordinary act of scholarship and storytelling to summon a moment that still echoes in the American soul. He turns Memphis itself into a kind of character, full of flaws and yearnings and aching hopes, as vividly rendered in Rosenbloom's hands as the great Martin King himself. As city and man wrestle toward their shared destinies, what takes shape is a masterpiece of narrative history. A deeply moving book."

—RON SUSKIND, Pulitzer Prize–winning journalist and author of *A Hope in the Unseen*

"Investigative journalist Rosenbloom reinforces the story of the end of Martin Luther King Jr.'s remarkable life with an integrated summary of the career that brought him finally to the Lorraine Motel in Memphis in spring 1968. . . . Rosenbloom also concisely describes the quotidian bonding of King and his diverse associates, and he doesn't ignore King's relationship with his wife, Coretta, as well as his extramarital adventures. The personality and moods— often dark, sometimes frolicsome—of the supremely gifted orator and preacher are a salient feature of the author's report. Also integral to the text are the . . . activities of King's feckless murderer, James Earl Ray. The portrayal of Ray in his perch watching the civil rights leader at the Lorraine Motel is succinctly cinematic. The previous night [King] mused on the possibility of a curtailed life, but, he said, he had 'been to the mountaintop.' . . . A skillful depiction of the people and the scenes surrounding the killing of the champion of the civil rights movement."

—*Kirkus Reviews*

Redemption

Redemption

Martin Luther King Jr.'s Last 31 Hours

– Joseph Rosenbloom –

Beacon Press
Boston

BEACON PRESS
Boston, Massachusetts
www.beacon.org

Beacon Press books
are published under the auspices of
the Unitarian Universalist Association of Congregations.

21 20 19 18   8 7 6 5 4 3 2 1

This book is printed on acid-free paper that meets the uncoated paper
ANSI/NISO specifications for permanence as revised in 1992.

Text design and composition by Kim Arney

Insert photo credits: Images 1, 2, 5, 6, and 11 © Ernest C. Withers Trust, courtesy Withers
Family Trust. Images 3, 4, 7, 8, 9, 10, 12, 13, 14, and 15 © Preservation and Special
Collections Department, University of Memphis Libraries.

Library of Congress Cataloging-in-Publication Data
Names: Rosenbloom, Joseph, author.
Title: Redemption : Martin Luther King Jr.'s last 31 hours / Joseph Rosenbloom.
Description: Boston : Beacon Press, [2018] | Includes bibliographical
    references and index. |
Identifiers: LCCN 2017024226 (print) | LCCN 2017029763 (ebook) |
    ISBN 9780807083406 (ebook) | ISBN 9780807083383 (hardcover : alk. paper)
Subjects: LCSH: King, Martin Luther, Jr., 1929-1968. | King, Martin Luther, Jr.,
    1929–1968—Assassination. | African Americans—Biography. | Civil rights workers—
    United States—Biography. | Baptists—United States—Clergy—Biography. | African
    Americans—Civil rights—History—20th century. | Civil rights movements—United
    States—History—20th century.
Classification: LCC E185.97.K5 (ebook) | LCC E185.97.K5 R598 2018 (print) |
    DDC 323.092 [B] —dc23
LC record available at https://lccn.loc.gov/2017024226

– Contents –

– Preface –

DURING THE SUMMER OF 1968 I had a reporter's internship at the *Commercial Appeal*, the morning daily in Memphis. The city was then trying to right itself from the shock and horror of the assassination, on April 4, of Martin Luther King Jr. In the newsroom, amid the cigarette smoke and brass spittoons, there was much talk about the events leading to King's murder. In my mind I filed away an idea. Someday, maybe, I would look into what happened in Memphis leading to the violent finale to King's life.

It took me forty years to get around to it. By then I had read a number of biographies of King. They typically included a chapter or two about his last days in Memphis. Some books scarcely dealt with King's presence in Memphis at all except as a backdrop to their actual subject: the story of King's assassin, James Earl Ray.

The books about Ray homed in on two questions: Why did he kill King? Did he conspire with others in a plot to assassinate him? Exhaustive investigations by the FBI, a task force of the Justice Department, the US House Select Committee on Assassinations, and authors such as George McMillan and Gerald Posner were never able to nail down a definite motive. Why Ray killed King probably will always remain a mystery. He was a virulent racist. Perhaps that was motive enough. The House panel relied on circumstantial evidence to conclude, vaguely, that there likely was a conspiracy. It pointed to Ray's brothers, John and Jerry, as possible coconspirators. But no clear-cut proof of a conspiracy has ever emerged.

The published accounts dealing with Memphis followed a broad story line. They told how, by April 1968, King was pursuing perhaps the most ambitious undertaking of his life, the Poor People's Campaign. No longer was he seeking only an end to racial segregation and discrimination, the cause that had consumed him for more than a decade. He was striving to end poverty in America, once and for all. He was mobilizing thousands of poor people to set up a shantytown in Washington, DC. He was vowing to lead his army of poor people for weeks, if not months, of civil disobedience in the streets and offices of federal lawmakers until they adopted a costly, sweeping antipoverty program.

When the biographies of King reached the chapters about Memphis, the story line centered on four consequential days: March 18 and 28 and April 3 and 4. He was in Memphis on March 18 to speak at a rally in support of a garbage workers' strike. On March 28 he was back in Memphis leading a pro-strike march, which turned into a riot. On April 3 he flew back, having resolved to organize a peaceful march. If he could stage a second march without another riot, he thought he could prove that his brand of nonviolent protest remained under his control. Unless he reasserted his leadership in that way, his plan to recruit a legion of poor people to protest nonviolently in the nation's capital was in jeopardy. Or so he reasoned. On April 4 he was murdered, snuffing out his plans for a redemptive march and the Poor People's Campaign.

I did not see any point in looking into the much-investigated question of whether Ray had conspired with others to kill King. I sensed that there was more to say about how events in Memphis might have conspired to obstruct King's plans as he returned to the city in 1968.

During a ten-year stint as a staff reporter for *Frontline*, the investigative documentary series on PBS, I developed a reflexive skepticism toward any supposed final word about a major public figure or event. Often the digging at *Frontline* uncovered new layers of revelation and understanding about stories that others had already put to bed. On that hunch I resolved to delve further into the Memphis story.

I had grown up relatively close, in Jackson, Tennessee. On visits to my family, I took the opportunity to stop by Memphis and continue my inquiry into King's last hours. I interviewed more than two dozen people who were either close to King or the events surrounding him in March and April 1968. Of course, I reviewed the vast trove of King-related files from sources such as the FBI and congressional investigators, as well as memoirs from King aides and confidants. Some of the material, surprisingly, was published or released as recently as 2012, such as the documents at the Woodruff Library at the Atlanta University Center and at Emory University.

A more complete picture of what happened to King in Memphis did indeed come into focus, along with some startling insights. It seems likely that Memphis and the Poor People's Campaign were linked in a way not previously revealed. King may have dramatized the garbage workers' strike in Memphis, at least in part, to drum up support for the Poor People's Campaign. By April 1968 the antipoverty operation was in great disarray, starved for funds and volunteers. A number of King's close aides strongly objected to his intervening in the Memphis strike. King may well have disregarded their advice not only because the strikers' cause was dear to him but also because of the urgency he felt to put the Poor People's Campaign back on track.

Venturing into Memphis not once or twice but three times was enormously risky. He knew little of the city's political and racial environment, yet he somehow reckoned that he could organize a peaceful march within a week in a strike-bound, riot-torn city on a razor's edge. He faced an implacable, sophisticated foe in Memphis mayor Henry Loeb. Most of all, King was raising his visibility as a highly controversial figure at a time when his opposition to the Vietnam War and promise of massive protest in the nation's capital already had made him a marked man in his own eyes.

It required extraordinary courage to return to Memphis and push ahead with the antipoverty campaign. It also reflected his growing impatience with capitalism and embrace of radical ideology in response to the urgent social and economic problems he perceived. That shift leftward seemed to seize him with greater passion by April 1968, an abrupt change in tone not fully documented in other accounts.

King was under enormous pressure from all sides in Memphis. He was exhausted from brutal days on the road proselytizing the Poor People's Campaign. He was contending with dissension within his staff and the broader civil rights movement and marital tensions at home. He had to confront a nettlesome Black Power faction in Memphis and an expected federal injunction barring him and seven members of his SCLC staff from leading another march in the city. He was fearful that he would die a violent death at any moment, as his last speech, the so-called "Mountaintop" speech on the evening of April 3, revealed so emotionally. The full story of King under the intense strain of Memphis paints a portrait of him in his last days that differs from the conventional view of him as master of his destiny.

The idea of redemption, as referenced in the book's title, *Redemption: Martin Luther King Jr.'s Last 31 Hours*, ties together three strands that defined the last phase of his life. He was trying to redeem his reputation as a nonviolent leader by leading a nonviolent march in Memphis. He was seeking an end of poverty to redeem what he regarded as the American promise of economic justice. He was drawing deeply on his faith in the redemptive power of sacrifice for a noble cause, as he risked his life—a faith rooted in the biblical example of Jesus.

Despite the many books already written about King, there seemed to be room for a concise story constructed around a narrative of the last thirty-one hours and twenty-eight minutes of his life. That is the span from the time King returned to Memphis on the morning of April 3 until his murder at 6:01 p.m. on April 4. Unlike the other books that cover King and Memphis, this one explores not just King's movements in Memphis but also Ray's during the same time period. It examines how a bumbling convict could have pulled off the assassination of the nation's foremost civil rights leader.

This book is, most of all, a close-up view of King as he struggled against enormous odds to end poverty in America. It is a view of him as he sought desperately to recover from a riot that threatened to subvert his impassioned cause, the Poor People's Campaign. Ultimately, he achieved redemption in the sense most important to him. He died sacrificing himself for the cause of social justice, in which he profoundly believed.

—Joseph Rosenbloom
June 19, 2017

Chapter 1

Atlanta Departure

*This is terrible. Now we'll never get
anybody to believe in nonviolence.*

—MLK, reacting to TV coverage of a riot that
erupted during a march he was leading
in Memphis, Tennessee, March 28, 1968

AT ABOUT NINE O'CLOCK on Wednesday morning, April 3, 1968, Martin Luther King Jr. boarded Eastern Air Lines Flight 381 in Atlanta. Along with four of his top aides he was flying to Memphis on an urgent mission.

King and his entourage of smartly dressed African Americans would have been an eye-catching sight for the forty-three other passengers on the airplane. With King were three men—Ralph Abernathy, Andrew Young, and Bernard Lee—and one woman, Dorothy Cotton. The men wore dark suits, white shirts, and muted neckties. Cotton was tastefully outfitted in a dignified dress, her hair smartly coiffed in a beehive. In style and demeanor, the five of them might have been a team of high-powered lawyers or corporate executives departing Atlanta on a business trip.

King would have attracted particular notice. A widely recognizable figure in 1968, he had been in the limelight since the heavily publicized Montgomery bus boycott twelve years before.

Anyone who remembered him as a young man first embracing the civil rights cause in the mid-1950s would have been shocked by the change in his appearance. In 1955 he was just twenty-six years old, recently hired—"called to the pulpit," as the expression had it—by the Dexter Avenue Baptist Church in Montgomery, Alabama. Photos from that period show him nattily garbed in a dark, loosely fitting suit, necktie, and fedora, a white handkerchief poking out of his jacket pocket. There was something about him then, the freshness of the face and the limpid softness of his eyes that conveyed a boyish innocence. It was easy to imagine him as a teenager outfitted in Easter finery for a service at the Ebenezer Baptist Church in Atlanta, where his father was the pastor.

Now, in 1968, he was a man in distress. His years in the movement had tested the limits of his courage and endurance. The strain had taken its toll emotionally and physically. He looked run-down, his eyes weary, face puffy, and neck straining against a white shirt collar.

He was dog-tired. He had been sleeping badly for weeks. He had been on the road drumming up support for the Poor People's Campaign, the mammoth antipoverty protest that was to commence in Washington in nineteen days.

He had left his house in Atlanta early that morning. His aide and dear friend Ralph Abernathy had driven to the modest redbrick house in the scruffy neighborhood of Vine City to pick him up. King's wife, Coretta, had offered the men a quick breakfast. No time to eat, they had told Coretta, not even accepting coffee and orange juice.[1]

Although he had scarcely caught his breath at home after two weeks of almost nonstop travel, he was traveling again. This time, though, he was not on another trip to recruit the thousands of poor people he intended to mobilize from around the country for weeks, or possibly months, of demonstrations in Washington.

He was bound for Memphis to lead a march the following Monday. In the spring of 1968 Memphis was a city in turmoil. A bitter strike by twelve hundred African American garbage workers had turned quickly into a racial firestorm. A pro-strike march under King's leadership six days earlier, on March 28, had spun out of control. Windows had been smashed, many downtown stores looted.

The stakes in Memphis were enormous for him and his movement. The fate of the Poor People's Campaign and, more broadly, his leadership of the civil rights movement were hanging in the balance. He was venturing back into a city reeling from the trauma of racial conflict and rioting. Even before the trouble in Memphis, his fear of being assassinated had been rattling him. Now he was being widely blamed and denounced for the riot, and the fear of a violent death preoccupied him all the more.

By speaking out sharply against the Vietnam War, as he had been doing for more than a year, he had plunged into a cauldron of controversy. His critics claimed that no true patriot could slam the nation's military engagement while hundreds of thousands of American troops were in harm's way. His plans for the Poor People's Campaign were arousing more hostility against him. He was threatening to plague lawmakers in Washington with militant civil disobedience until they committed the federal government to an immense program to end poverty. To many Americans he was a radical, a threat to civil order. Many believed he was leading the country into an abyss of strife and chaos. By inserting himself into the Memphis strike, resulting in a march turned riotous, he had aggravated the fears. Now he was returning to Memphis to lead another march and restore his credibility as a nonviolent leader. It would expose him to greater controversy, greater risk. Fearful, but courageous in his resolve, he was flying to Memphis, come what may.

The Tennessee city, as Mark Twain wrote in 1882, was "nobly situated on a commanding bluff" overlooking the majestic Mississippi River.[2] For the 60 percent of whites among its total population of six hundred thousand, Memphis had a long, noble tradition, and not just in geography. For them Memphis was a proud Southern city of well-attended churches and well-tended lawns, a paragon of order and civility. At the junction of northwestern Mississippi, Southwestern Arkansas, and southeastern Tennessee, the city stood as the gateway to the Deep South, and it reflected much of that region's gracious character.

For blacks it was a very different story. Gradual desegregation had been under way since the early 1960s, but the city was still largely divided into two cultures, a dominant class of whites and a subservient class of blacks. The garbage strike, which had begun on February 12, had cast the depth of the racial divide into bold relief. Local historian Joan Beifuss would write that the conflict over the strike had quickly stripped away "the thin veneer of dialogue and handshakes and politeness and kindly interest" and exposed such a "depth of ill will" and "intensity of hostility" as to declare that "the bitterness had always lain somewhere close to the surface."[3]

The black community had rallied behind the strike. Henry Loeb, the newly elected white mayor, had the strong backing of the white establishment against the strike, and he had taken a hard line against it. As garbage piled up and the strikers staged demonstrations against Loeb's hiring of replacement workers, tensions mounted by the day.

King had spoken for the first time in support of the strike at a rally on March 18. He had come back to Memphis ten days later to lead a march. He had been expecting the march to proceed lawfully through downtown streets. Barely had the march begun when it turned violent. Police responded with clubs, tear gas, and guns. Four looters were shot, one fatally. Five police officers were hospitalized, and about sixty other people received medical care for their injuries.[4]

Splashed on newspapers and TV screens around the country, the story of the Memphis riot was big news. King was outspoken in deploring the violence, which he attributed to a small number of young rowdies who had tagged along behind the great throng of peaceful marchers. At a news conference the next day, he told a reporter for the *Commercial Appeal* that he had been blindsided. He said that he had had no warning about the potential for violence and had "no part in the planning of the march. Our intelligence was totally nil." King went on to fault the police for having dealt brutally with many marchers.[5]

But his credibility as a nonviolent leader who could keep the movement free of violence was under fierce attack. There were potshots from segregationists like Robert Byrd of West Virginia. While not surprising, the invective from the right had more bite than usual. Byrd, then one of the most zealous segregationists in the US Senate, assailed King as a "self-seeking rabble rouser," as quoted in an FBI memo. If King were allowed to "rabble-rouse" in Washington as he threatened, Byrd declared, the city "may well be treated to the same kind of violence, destruction, looting and bloodshed" that had erupted in Memphis.

The *Commercial Appeal* echoed Byrd with a scalding editorial on March 30: "Dr. King's pose as a leader of a non-violent movement has been shattered. He now has the entire nation doubting his word when he insists that his April project—a shanty-town sit-in in the nation's capital—can be peaceful." A more sympathetic newspaper, the *New York Times*, cautioned King in its editorial on the same day against engaging in "emotional demonstrations in this time of civic unrest."

Worse, King had to contend with spasms of doubt from within the civil rights movement. In 1963 Adam Clayton Powell, the first African American elected to Congress from New York, had hailed him as "probably the greatest human being in the United States today."[6] Now he mocked him as Martin "Loser" King.[7] Responding to a reporter's question about the violent eruption in Memphis, Roy Wilkins, the influential head of the National Association for the Advancement of Colored People, commented about the upcoming antipoverty campaign: "The great danger of Dr. King's demonstration is that he might not be able to keep control of it." Privately Wilkins was saying that King ought to cut his losses and scrap the Poor People's Campaign altogether.[8]

King himself had his doubts. Like Wilkins, he pondered whether he ought to call the whole Washington thing off. Wouldn't the rioting in Memphis and attacks against King blunt poor people's interest in joining the Washington demonstrations? "They will hold back if they think they will be in a campaign that will be taken over by violent elements," King confided to a close adviser.[9] In his despair King thought perhaps he should fast in a show of penance. Ultimately, he did not fast, but he seriously considered it.

If King's energy on the road had seemed inexhaustible for many years, it was no longer so. Like any flesh-and-blood mortal, he could not maintain his punishing schedule of speaking engagements and almost incessant travel without a physical cost.

He was pushing himself to the brink of collapse. His doctors had hospitalized him or ordered him to days of bed rest for exhaustion on at least four occasions over the previous four years (in October 1964, February 1965, August 1966, and April 1967).[10] By February 1968, the rush to organize the antipoverty campaign was wearing him down to such an alarming extent that he reluctantly heeded his doctor's advice to rest. Along with Ralph Abernathy, he took a one-week break to recuperate in Acapulco.[11]

It was not only sheer exhaustion that accounted for King's sinking spirits. His influence as a political and moral force had peaked in the mid-sixties. He was then riding the crest of a series of triumphs: the electrifying "I Have a Dream" speech during the March on Washington of 1963; the Nobel Peace Prize bestowed on him the next year; and the landmark desegregation and voting-rights legislation enacted by Congress in 1964 and 1965.

His best years seemed behind him. His venture into the more complex racial and political minefield of Chicago had stalled. Rioting was plaguing the nation's inner cities, as though defying his nonviolent leadership. Young Black Power militants had captured the dynamism of the movement. By 1968 it seemed that he was "old news," as his friend and financial backer Harry Belafonte would note in a memoir.[12] The book King published six months earlier, *Where Do We Go from Here: Chaos or Community?*, sold poorly, and many reviewers panned it.[13] For the first time in a decade the name of Martin Luther King Jr. did not appear on the Gallup Poll annual list of the ten most admired Americans.[14]

The turn of events in Memphis was propelling King back into front-page news, abruptly and disastrously. The torrent of adverse publicity was sapping his usual optimism, testing his resilience. "He was very, terribly depressed, a depression that I had never experienced before, and had never seen," Abernathy would recall.[15] Somehow over two soul-searching days back in Atlanta, King overcame the gloom, determined to move ahead. He would not yield to despair. He was returning to Memphis, resolved to lead a corrective march untainted by violence. Or so he desperately hoped.

Once aboard the Eastern jet to Memphis, King and his four aides sat close together. King and Dorothy Cotton were in adjoining seats. Hardly had they settled down before the pilot announced, "I have to ask everyone to leave the plane because Dr. King and some of his staff are on the plane and there has been a bomb threat," as Cotton recounted years later.[16]

A wave of fear rippled through the plane, launching the passengers to their feet. "When the pilot made that announcement, we stood up," Cotton continued, "and I was moving really rather energetically, and I stepped on Martin's foot. I said, 'Don't you think we should move it? There has been a bomb scare,' and he sort of glared at me."[17]

As the other passengers surged down the aisle, King barely moved. Rather than rush off the plane, King "pulled back and let people get off," Young recalled. That was not how Bernard Lee, who served King as a sort of aide-de-camp and unarmed bodyguard, reacted. Lee hastened toward the exit. He was "the first one off the plane," said Young. The sight of his bodyguard leaving him behind in that moment of danger had King smiling. It was a moment that he would later play for laughs.[18]

King's nonchalance did not surprise Young. Threats against King's life were an almost constant menace. King had a stock reply to reports of death threats against him. He would say that he received them every day, and he could not worry about them, because no one could stop attempts on his life.

Once King and the other passengers disembarked from the plane, police officers brought dogs aboard to sniff for bombs. A thorough check found nothing suspicious. After an hour's delay the passengers returned to their seats. King turned to Abernathy. "Well," he said wryly, "it looks like they won't kill me this flight."[19]

Chapter 2

Detour

And I submit this afternoon that we can end poverty in the United States. Our nation has the resources to do it.

—MLK, speech at Stanford University, April 14, 1967

KING MIGHT HAVE returned to Memphis earlier in his quest to save his reputation. But a critical speaking obligation stood in the way. On March 31, three days before leaving for Memphis, he was in Washington, DC, delivering the Sunday sermon at the Washington National Cathedral. His remarks centered on the Vietnam War and the Poor People's Campaign, though the crisis in Memphis must have been weighing heavily on him.

The storied cathedral offered him a platform for reaching the political elite of the nation's capital. It was an occasion to build support for his stands against the war and for far-reaching federal antipoverty legislation. Sunday sermons, of course, were routine for King. So was the mixing of religion and politics whenever he preached themes of social justice.

But this time he was mixing two causes, both hurtling him deeply into two bitter national debates and blurring his image as the nation's foremost champion of racial desegregation. His high visibility as a zealous foe of the US policy in Vietnam exposed him to attacks on grounds that he had no business expounding on military matters. The plan to besiege the nation's capital in the name of ending poverty was causing even many of his supporters to reassess their opinions of him.

The Poor People's Campaign would be like no other he had undertaken. A legion of volunteers would stage weeks, possibly months, of "militant" demonstrations in Washington until lawmakers enacted far-reaching programs for the poor. He was threatening epic disruption of the federal government. The massive civil disobedience King envisioned was bound to lead to scuffles with police at the least, and possibly violent confrontation, along with the almost certain arrest of hundreds, perhaps thousands, of people.

The siege of Washington by hordes of poor people would intensify the heat in a political climate already at the boiling point because of the Vietnam War. Multitudes of demonstrators against the war were taking to the streets of Washington and other cities around the country chanting, "Hey! Hey! LBJ! How many kids did you kill today?" Senator Eugene McCarthy of Minnesota was drawing widespread support in his bid to unseat President Johnson by running for the Democratic presidential nomination on an antiwar platform. In the New Hampshire primary McCarthy won more than two-fifths of the vote against an incumbent president in his own party. Johnson was under intense pressure to withdraw US troops from Vietnam or resign. Johnson buckled, announcing on March 31 he would not seek reelection as president in 1968.

Earlier on that day, an overflow crowd had gathered in the neo-Gothic splendor of the National Cathedral to hear King speak. He must have sensed that many of his listeners in that Episcopal sanctum lived apart from America's poor and knew little of them. He beseeched them to consider the plight of America's forty million "poverty stricken" people, who, he said, were "invisible" in a country that is "so rich" that many "don't see the poor."[1] Within a few miles of Congress and the White House, his booming voice ringing with indignation, he demanded urgent federal action against poverty.

Turning to Vietnam, he decried it as one of the most "unjust wars" ever.[2] Eloquent, emotional, and powerful, the sermon evoked King's passion for the antipoverty and antiwar causes that he had made his own by the spring of 1968.

On the road when he was in Washington and elsewhere he carried a well-stuffed briefcase, which served him as a kind of traveling file cabinet containing materials to inform him on war, poverty, and other issues. It was a rectangular briefcase, emblazoned with the initials MLK in gold above the latch. It included a few personal effects: a tin of aspirin, a bottle of Alka Seltzer, and a can of shaving powder. It was crammed with papers and two books written by him.

Among the papers were at least two items that indicated the breadth of his curiosity. One was a speech by ecologist Hugo Boyko evaluating the potential for Israeli-Arab cooperation in food production. Another was a newspaper article about Florida governor Claude Kirk Jr.'s private police force. The oldest papers dated back to 1966. The Vietnam War figures in several newspaper articles from that year.[3]

A six-page statement that King released to the public in October 1966 set forth his view of Black Power, the slogan adopted by young militants such as Stokely Carmichael and H. Rap Brown to dramatize their call for aggressive methods to advance civil rights. The statement reflected the fine line that King was walking on the subject. It disavowed the slogan Black Power for its "connotations of violence and separatism." But it sympathized with the "unendurable frustrations" of people of his race who were "taunted by empty promises, humiliated and deprived by the filth and decay" of America's slums.[4]

Buried in his traveling case was a two-year-old article from the *Wall Street Journal* about a federal study warning of potential "Watts-type violence" in twenty-one cities. (The 1965 riot in the Watts section of Los Angeles had left 34 dead, 947 injured, and $45 million in property damage.[5] More civil unrest had flared up in dozens of cities over the next two years. Some of the worst rioting was in the slums of Newark and Detroit. Whole neighborhoods were devastated by widespread looting and violence that left scores dead and many hundreds injured during the summer of 1967.)

Also tucked into the briefcase was a book of King's sermons, *Strength to Love*, and his fifth and last book, *Where Do We Go from Here*. The last book ponders the state of the movement ("Negroes have established a foothold, no more") and appeals for a great federal commitment to end poverty.[6] King devoted a fifty-eight-page chapter of the book, the longest, to the subject of Black Power. In the second-longest chapter, he examined the related development of "white backlash," the reaction of white people so alarmed by the urban violence that they were demanding harsh law-and-order measures. King was unsympathetic. He wrote that the backlash sprang either from whites' racism or a lack of empathy for the "ache and anguish" of daily life in the ghetto.[7]

Tellingly, King had in his traveling file pages 179 and 180 of *Where Do We Go from Here*, printed out on separate sheets of paper. On those pages he discusses two parallel "revolutions." One is in technology, the other in the civil rights and anticolonial movements sweeping the globe. Both revolutions King sees as progressing with inevitability. In reflecting about that point later on, he must have mused about how to make the issue of poverty relevant to all people. In the margin of page 180, he had scribbled in blue ink, "The agony of the poor impoverishes the rich. The betterment of the poor enriches the rich. We are inevitably our brother's keeper because we are our brother's brother. Whatever affects one affects all."

That he was carrying a copy of *Where Do We Go from Here* with him, along with his markup of pages from the book, seems to underscore how intensely he had turned to poverty as a transcendent issue. His pivot from the decade-long pursuit of racial progress to the larger issues of poverty and war marked his most dramatic turning point as a national leader.

Some papers in the briefcase harked back to important public pronouncements of the mid-sixties. On April 4, 1967, at Riverside Church in New York he had delivered a speech on Vietnam that had attracted wide public attention. He meant the speech to be a definitive statement of his views on the subject. He denounced Lyndon Johnson's policy as morally unjust and strategically flawed. He said the war was draining the US treasury of money that could have funded antipoverty programs and that it was impressing black soldiers into Vietnam service in disproportionate numbers. He deplored the death and destruction it was inflicting on Vietnam and its people. No one concerned about "the integrity and life of America today," he thundered, "can ignore the present war. If America's soul becomes totally poisoned, part of the autopsy must read Vietnam."[8]

As for the rioting in Watts and other cities, King looked at the urban strife as a product of poverty and the associated ills of unemployment, blighted housing, and shoddy public education. To respond to Black Power, King was rolling out the Poor People's Campaign as a massive, militant, though nonviolent, alternative.

Even King's support of the strike in Memphis, a labor dispute between the city and municipal employees, was supposed to advance the Poor People's Campaign. As King noted when he addressed the pro-strike rally in Memphis on March 18, the paycheck of the garbage workers was so paltry that some had turned to food stamps to feed their families. Linking their plight to the wider issue of American poverty would dramatize his case for the Washington protest.

King envisioned Memphis as a springboard to Washington. Instead, the woeful turn of events—the rioting that marred his pro-strike march of March 28 and the imperative to recover by staging a nonviolent march on April 6—was having the opposite effect. Returning to Memphis now would be a costly detour. It would bog King and his staff down for at least five days in a city roiled by racial conflict. They would be stuck there until at least the day of the redemptive march, set for Monday, April 8.

The timing could hardly have been worse. King and his aides were in the final stage of recruiting volunteers for the Poor People's Campaign. They had a monumental task ahead of them. They were seeking an ethnically diverse cross section of poor people from ten cities in the Northeast and Midwest and from small towns and rural areas in five southern states. The African American preacher who grew up in middle-class circumstances in Atlanta was summoning poor people from across America. He was calling to Washington—in his terminology—not only Negroes but also Appalachian whites, Mexican Americans, Puerto Ricans, and American Indians.

He was promising a "massive mobilization." It would mean flooding Washington with protesters, settling them in makeshift tent cities on the grounds of the Washington Monument or Lincoln Memorial. If their extensive demands for antipoverty legislation were not met, he would dispatch the protesters en masse into streets, parks, and office buildings. The protesters would jam the halls of Congress and offices of executive departments, swarm into hospital emergency rooms, and quite possibly tie up the vehicular traffic of central Washington. When asked by a reporter about the latter tactic, King was evasive. But he was clear about his intentions: the protesters would "plague" Washington as long as necessary to achieve their goals.[9]

To prepare for an operation of that scale, King was shifting the Southern Christian Leadership Conference onto a different track. He had founded the SCLC, in 1957, in alliance with a regional network of mostly Baptist ministers, to struggle against racial segregation in the South. Now the emphasis would fall squarely on economic justice. He reassigned his staff to concentrate on the profuse details of the antipoverty drive. They would help recruit and train the thousands of people in the discipline of nonviolence. They would plan and execute the complex logistics to transport, house, feed, and manage the great mass of protesters.

That was the plan before the debacle in Memphis. Diverting to Memphis for damage control was throwing the Poor People's Campaign off schedule. As originally conceived, the plan was to enlist a first wave of three thousand poor people to converge on Washington in early April. Thousands more would follow in later months. Hastily revised because of the detour to Memphis, the plan was now for the campaign to begin on April 22. The aim was to draw not thousands but only a "symbolic delegation" to Washington at that time, as the *Commercial Appeal* reported on March 30.

Recruiting volunteers, whose bodies and honor would be on the line in Washington, would have been hard enough if the Memphis riot had not undercut King's image as an apostle of nonviolence. Now he believed he had to restore his credibility in order to reassure volunteers. If not, he feared few people would follow him to the nation's capital.

King's powerful oratory, his iconic stature as the personification of the civil rights movement, the respect and awe with which millions of disadvantaged Americans regarded him—they were the engine behind the Poor People's Campaign. On his personal magnetism hinged the success of his appeal for volunteers as he traveled around the country to build support. Without that central pillar of his credibility solidly in place, King acknowledged that the Washington campaign was "doomed."[10]

His breakneck schedule in March 1968 allowed him to stump from town to town, city to city, pleading for volunteers. During the eight days that ended March 18, he delivered thirty-five speeches at stops from Michigan to California. The schedule for a single day, March 19, sounded like the bookings of a week or two for gospel singers on a Delta tour. Starting in the early morning, he crisscrossed a large swath of Mississippi. He spoke at small African American churches in Batesville, Marks, Clarksdale, Greenwood, Grenada, and Laurel, finally reaching Hattiesburg and a bed close to midnight.

Marks, Mississippi, would play a special role. It was to be the jumping-off point for a mule train that would plod the one thousand miles to Washington as a sort of moving billboard to promote the antipoverty cause. In his sermon at the National Cathedral he singled out Marks as an example of the privation that had inspired him to launch the Washington campaign. It was a backwater Delta town of twenty-six hundred inhabitants in Quitman County, one of the poorest counties in the United States. At the edge of cotton fields, he said, he had seen "hundreds of little black boys and girls walking the streets with no shoes to wear" and heard stories from jobless mothers and fathers about times when they could survive only if they would "go around to the neighbors and ask them for a little something."[11]

In his travels to rally poor people to Washington, King barnstormed from one small airport to another in a chartered, twin-engine Cessna 40. King and a few aides then would rush to a nearby African American church where he would speak. Even with the benefit of a private plane, they sometimes arrived hours behind schedule.

After Mississippi they moved on to Alabama and Georgia. He would talk to whatever crowd waited long enough to hear him. King would call on the people who turned out, as he did in Waycross, Georgia, on March 22, to join the "powerful and meaningful" Washington campaign that, he promised, would cause the "walls of injustice to come tumbling down." His voice would resound with emotional fervor, attuned to the religious convictions of his listeners. In Waycross he hit that pious note, saying that poor people, as God's children, were no less deserving than other Americans of jobs and income.[12]

If it had not been for the quagmire of Memphis, King's schedule would have had him presiding over a meeting of the national steering committee of the Poor People's Campaign in Atlanta on April 1.[13]

That meeting had been called off. Further, he would have been in Chicago on April 3, the day he was now flying to Tennessee instead, and in Detroit the next day. Now he would have to scrub travel to both cities. The detour to Memphis was bleeding time and energy that King and his staff had intended to devote to the antipoverty drive at a critical stage.

The top echelon of his staff flying with him that morning from Atlanta to Memphis had major assignments as area managers of the Poor People's Campaign. Abernathy had three cities under his watch, Washington, Baltimore, and Newark, New Jersey, Young had New York City and Philadelphia, and Cotton had North Carolina and Virginia.

Other key aides—Jesse Jackson, James Bevel, James Orange, and Hosea Williams—were already in Memphis, having arrived earlier in the week. All would have to suspend their work on the antipoverty campaign. Williams had a particularly vital role as the national field director overseeing the entire campaign. King's aides did not want to pause the antipoverty campaign and come to Memphis. They relented only at King's insistence. Ordinarily they would have held workshops and planning sessions for many weeks, if not months, to pull off a protest of that magnitude. Preparing for the Birmingham campaign had consumed three months of planning and training. In Memphis they would have five days.

King disregarded not just his aides' advice but also the pleadings of Marian Logan, a trusted SCLC board member on whom he relied for counsel and emotional support. On the night of March 28, still reeling from the day's riot, King had called Logan at her apartment in New York City. When she heard that he was stranded in Memphis, she winced. She told him bluntly, as she would recall, "You ought to get your ass out of Memphis."

King replied, "Darling, we can't turn around now. We have to keep going."[14]

Chapter 3

The Strike

*We have thousands and thousands of Negroes
working on full-time jobs with part-time income.*

—MLK, speaking at an SCLC retreat
in Atlanta, January 15, 1968

THE STRIKE THAT BROUGHT King to Memphis in 1968 began on February 12. The date coincided with Abraham Lincoln's birthday. The timing was accidental. As the strike's leaders initially conceived it, the walkout had nothing to do with race—no symbolic link to the Great Emancipator.

The workers struck for the usual reasons: better wages and working conditions and union recognition. Yet what began purely as a labor dispute swiftly assumed the proportions of a highly charged racial confrontation, as labor historian Michael K. Honey explains in his definitive book about the Memphis strike.[1] Just four days into the strike, the Memphis chapter of the NAACP thrust race to the front and center. At a news conference NAACP officials decried "racial discrimination" in the city's treatment of the garbage workers.

Within a few weeks, the men on strike were carrying signs reading, "I AM A MAN." As a rallying cry, the slogan might have seemed oddly mild. Yet it evoked an anguished plea for an end to the era in which Southerners assumed the right to address adult black men as "boys" and lorded over them as if they had no more rights than boys.[2] Taylor Rogers, who was in his tenth year as a garbage worker before going on strike in 1968, would put it years later: "We wanted some dignity. We wanted to be treated like men. We were tired of being treated like boys."[3]

The NAACP played no part in initiating the strike, only in backing it once it began. To the Reverend Samuel "Billy" Kyles, a Baptist minister and prominent member of the NAACP in Memphis, the strike came as a complete surprise. The garbage workers belonged to a world apart from the NAACP.

They were not part of the city's African American elite, the ministers, lawyers, and other professionals. The NAACP was in the hands of the elite. In the early 1960s, it turned to the federal judiciary for progress on civil rights. It brought lawsuits seeking court orders to desegregate schools, parks, and other public facilities. In some instances it engaged in sit-ins and picketing. But the NAACP leaders conducted their protests quietly, respectfully, collaboratively.

To see a movie at a segregated Malco theater, Kyles, a film buff, would have had to climb a fire escape stairway and sit in the balcony section for African Americans (the "buzzard's roost," he called it). He refused. Instead he called M. A. Lightman, owner of the Malco. Kyles and Lightman devised a scheme to desegregate the theater quietly. Kyles and his wife slipped into the whites-only section for a midday showing of *To Kill a Mockingbird*. There were about a dozen whites in the theater. "I don't think they even knew [the sit-in] was happening," Kyles would recount. The Malco, bowing to the new reality, announced that the days of segregation in its movie theaters were over. As a token of his appreciation for how gracefully Kyles had desegregated his theater, Lightman presented him with a gift: a one-year pass to the Malco.[4]

Kyles did not imagine the garbage workers as likely instigators of a civil rights protest. He doubted that they had the wherewithal to defy the city's white establishment. They were the "lowest on the totem pole," as Kyles put it.[5] They inhabited a world of foul-smelling waste and low social status. They lacked education, money, and political power. They were ushers in Kyles's church, not deacons.

One leader of the garbage workers' union was forty-six-year-old Joe Warren. At six foot one, broad-shouldered, a combat veteran of World War II, Warren was not a man to trifle with. He had grown up on a farm near the impoverished farming hamlet of Cordova, ten miles east of Memphis. The black farmers who populated the Cordova area hitched their hopes to the cotton crop. They were mostly sharecroppers who rented land on credit to grow cotton and borrowed from the landowner to buy supplies. They repaid their debt by committing to the landlord a share of their cotton sales. As the system played out, it was "arbitrary and highly susceptible to exploitation," writes Eugene Dattel in his economic history of cotton and race.[6] It was, in effect, a system of post-slavery peonage. It kept many of Warren's neighbors in perpetual poverty.

Warren's father, McKinley Warren, was not a sharecropper. He owned a twenty-three-acre farm. But he, his wife (Estelle), and three children endured much the same hardscrabble conditions as their sharecropping neighbors.[7] The Warrens lived in a two-room, log-and-plank house practically next to the tracks of the Nashville, Chattanooga, and St. Louis Railroad.

By age ten Joe was driving mules to plow the fields and picking cotton under the broiling Tennessee sun. It was backbreaking work: bending over, plucking the fiber from its prickly, three-lobed bolls, tugging a long sack between rows, and tediously, interminably stuffing the cotton fluff into the sack. To earn more, Joe quit school in the eighth grade so that he could work longer hours in the fields.

Weary of the farm life, venturing into an unknown and uncertain world, he fled to the city down the road but an eternity away: Memphis. Displaced by cotton-picking machines and other automated equipment in the 1930s and 1940s, many rural blacks like Warren were quitting farm life and heading to Memphis and cities beyond. Jobs were scarce in the cities for low-skilled farmhands, and racial barriers severely limited the prospects for decent employment. Warren, who was just sixteen, landed a laborer's job at the Buckeye Cotton Oil Company.

Though he was barely literate and had a criminal record—a juvenile conviction for stealing tires off a truck—the army drafted him for service during World War II. He saw fierce combat in Italy as a rifleman with the Ninety-Seventh Infantry. Except for having a front tooth knocked out during one firefight, he survived unscathed. "Thank God, I didn't get killed," he would say. He was honorably discharged in 1945 as a staff sergeant. In his separation papers the army recognized him for having "placed fire on the enemy, assisting in the capture of an enemy position. Fired rifle, threw grenades. Fired bazooka and A-30 caliber machine gun. Assisted in the capture of enemy positions and personnel."

He returned home to find the racial chasm in Memphis as wide as ever. "Couldn't even talk to a white woman," he would recall.[8] He went to work as a custodian at the Firestone Tire and Rubber Company plant. Laid off in 1962 with few options for employment, he took a job as a garbage-truck driver for the Memphis Department of Public Works.

"Tub toters" was then a common name for garbagemen. It was a reference to the tin tubs that they would hoist on their shoulders, carry to backyards, fill with garbage, and lug to the trucks. The tubs leaked water, garbage, and maggots through holes in the bottom. As Taylor Rogers, who had been a tub toter, would say years later, "You didn't have nowhere to wash your hands. You'd stand beside the truck and eat your lunch. It was just pure hell."[9]

To cover the prescribed routes, Warren and Rogers sometimes had to stay on the job past their forty-hour workweek. There was no pay for overtime work. No unemployment insurance. No disability benefits. There was an optional life insurance policy and a pension plan. But the workers' share of the cost was such that almost no one signed up for either.[10]

Pay was low. In 1968 the average was $1.80 an hour, fifteen cents above the minimum wage. Starting pay was $1.65, which an article on February 23 in the *Commercial Appeal* said roughly matched what other southern cities paid garbage workers. For those who were supporting a wife and several children, however, it was not a living wage.[11] In his Memphis speech of March 18, King would drive the point home, saying that it was a travesty for full-time workers to receive part-time wages.[12]

By and by, Warren was grumbling openly to his fellow workers about their working conditions and low pay. Warren found a ready ear in a coworker, Thomas Oliver "T. O." Jones. Like Warren, Jones was a World War II veteran—in his case, having served in the navy. At war's end, Jones found work in a unionized shipyard at Oakland, California. In 1958, he returned to his hometown of Memphis and took a job as a garbageman.[13]

Mindful how unions could improve the lot of workers, Jones soon began organizing one to represent employees of the city's Department of Public Works. He tapped Warren to help. Jones and Warren persuaded hundreds of their coworkers to join them. Identified by DPW management as a union firebrand, Jones was fired in 1963, but that did not stop his drive to establish a union. In 1964, he and Warren persuaded the garbage collectors to form Local 1733 of the American Federation of State, County, and Municipal Employees—AFSCME. Backed by the power of an emerging union, the workers won modest concessions. Wage increases of a few cents an hour were granted each year. Uniforms and foul-weather gear were provided. The tin tubs were phased out in favor of three-wheel pushcarts. A grievance procedure was instituted.[14] The city adopted a civil service policy providing vacations and sick leave.[15]

Unchanged was a deep-seated racial bias. The men who hauled the garbage were black. The supervisors were white. A black worker stayed on the payroll at the mercy of his white supervisors. Warren would recall: "The bosses would fire you if they wanted to fire you."[16]

For Warren and Jones, the key to the union's survival was union recognition and a dues checkoff, whereby the city would deduct union dues from its members' paychecks for transfer to the union treasury. Without the dues checkoff, a great majority of union members declined to pay the $4-a-month dues. If they did so, many of them feared, it would mark them as union activists and cost them their jobs.

When Memphis businessman Henry Loeb announced that he would run for mayor in 1967, it seemed to present the union with an opportunity. On July 4, 1967, Warren called on Loeb at his stately house on Colonial Drive. He had a proposition: if Loeb would agree to recognize the union and allow a dues checkoff, the union would endorse him for mayor. Years later, Warren would remember the mayor's curt reply: "There has never been a public employees' union in this city, and there never will be."[17]

Loeb won the election anyway without the union's support. Warren and Jones determined they had no recourse except to strike. They thought it best to wait until Loeb completed his first few months in office, his honeymoon period. Perhaps they would strike in the summer of 1968. Then, in the heat of the Memphis sun, piles of fast-rotting and stinking garbage would accumulate all over town. In those circumstances the mayor would feel greater pressure to settle a work stoppage on favorable terms for the union.

Back-to-back events on two successive days in early 1968 triggered a premature strike. On January 31, twenty-two black sewer and drain workers were sent home when it began to rain. No white employees were sent home. When the rain stopped a couple of hours later, the whites began working. They earned a full day's pay. The blacks complained, and the city eventually agreed to pay them, but only for two hours.

On the very next day, a five-man garbage crew was caught in a driving rainstorm. There was room for only three of them in the cab of their Weiner barrel truck. The two junior men, Echol Cole and Robert Walker, sought refuge in back. They crawled into the yawning compactor compartment. A freak electrical short apparently caused by an errant shovel hitting loose wires triggered the compactor. Cole and Walker were dragged into its jaws and crushed to death.

The nightmarish accident buttressed the workers' long-standing complaint about outdated and derelict equipment. The city had introduced the barrel truck only ten years earlier in grudging compliance with the workers' demands. A compactor-equipped truck was a modernizing step forward. But the barrel trucks posed new hazards. They were not always well maintained. Union leaders had been pleading with the city to replace them, according to local historian Joan Beifuss.[18]

Aggrieved and outraged by two jarring events—the rainy day incident and the horrible deaths of Cole and Walker—Local 1733 voted to strike. The union's members vowed not to return to work until Loeb granted their demands. For workers who risked their jobs and the livelihoods of their families by striking, it was a great leap. Taylor Rogers, who was supporting a family of eight children, five girls and three boys, remembered the wrenching moment: "I sat down and talked to my family before I went out on strike. They said, 'look, Daddy, you ain't doing nothing no way.' . . . And my boy say, 'Daddy, we're with you. We'll go out and work and whatever money we get, we'll bring in.'" Once the strike was under way, the son, Taylor Jr., shined shoes to help out.[19]

The early days of the work stoppage went exceedingly well. By the third day the strike was idling all but four of the city's 188 garbage trucks. Thirteen hundred employees of the Department of Public Works, all African Americans, were refusing to work. On the fourth day, Joseph Paisley, an AFSCME organizer in Tennessee, crowed to a reporter: "They stood in unison, one thousand plus, they're not going back."[20]

Mayor Loeb, however, was not about to sit on his hands as garbage stacked up throughout his city. One week into the strike, Loeb began hiring workers to replace the strikers. Fearful of losing their jobs permanently and with rent and car payments coming due, some of the strikers were drifting back to work. By mid-March, a month after the strike began, the *Commercial Appeal* would report that sixty-seven trucks were back in service.

Working overtime, escorted by police squad cars, hastily mobilized crews were collecting garbage from most of the city's businesses and apartment buildings. As though to demonstrate a civic duty to counter the strike, Boy

Scouts were pitching in to haul away some of the garbage heaps in residential neighborhoods.

By April, ninety-five garbage trucks were rumbling through the city's streets.[21] The trucks, crewed mostly by new hires, were steadily clearing mounds of accumulated garbage from alleys, sidewalks, and yards. The number of trucks back in service amounted to only half the pre-strike level. That was enough, though, to relieve the pressure on Mayor Loeb.

Chapter 4

Airport Arrival

The Movement lives or dies in Memphis.

—MLK, speaking to his staff,
Atlanta, March 30, 1968

A CROWD AT GATE 17 of the Memphis airport was waiting for King's delayed flight from Atlanta on Wednesday morning, April 3. In the welcoming party of about sixty were African American ministers, civil rights activists, and union leaders. There was a gaggle of news reporters, some shouldering TV cameras. Spilling into the hallway were dozens of curious outbound passengers. They stopped in their tracks to gawk.

King's jet arrived at 10:33 a.m., as bursts of sunshine warmed the city. A photo published the next day in the *Memphis Press-Scimitar*, the afternoon daily, shows him and three of his aides on the airport tarmac. Overcoats draped over their arms, the aides hurry along. King seems to be hanging back, peering upward to his left, eyes narrowed, lips pursed. He looks wary, somber. In his white shirt and dark suit, the jacket tidily buttoned, he seems like a man with all under control except for the worry on his face.

Had his circumstances been different, the weather might have lifted his spirits. He was arriving in early spring. The temperature was in the upper sixties, though rain and a cold front were expected later in the day. Easter was eleven days away.

The sprawling city then stretched eastward almost to cotton fields. Westward was the downtown bluff near the swirling junction of the Mississippi and Wolf Rivers. Already Memphis was teeming with spring colors.

Daffodils were peaking, bright yellow. The azaleas were a blaze of red, white, and purple. In sync with the flowers, ads in the two Memphis dailies were brimming with Easter sales offering pastel dresses and ornate bonnets.

The rhythm of life seemed utterly normal in other ways. Movie theaters were open for business. Hometown boy Elvis Presley had top billing in *Stay Away, Joe*, at the State, in which he played an Indian rodeo hand returning to the reservation to "raise the very devil with women," as one reviewer wrote. In their nonstop Elvis watch, Memphis newspapers were reporting that he was in residence at Graceland with his wife, Priscilla, and their newborn daughter, Lisa Marie.

The annual Cotton Carnival was on the calendar, the city's premier high-society event, a five-day extravaganza in late May. Exclusive secret societies were already doing their part by anointing faux-royalty from among the city's social elite. Indeed, the Nineteenth Century Club and the Petroleum Club were each disclosing their picks for prince and princess. The princesses, all college students or fresh graduates, resplendent in white dresses and bejeweled crowns, would be riding through downtown streets on parade floats later that spring.

As the garbage workers' strike entered its fifty-first day, however, no one could say that all was normal in Memphis. In many neighborhoods trash bags littered the sidewalks. Whole blocks of the downtown were in shambles from the riot of March 28. Store windows were shattered. Shelves were bare from looting.

Only a few of the thirty-eight hundred National Guard troops that patrolled the city after the riot remained on duty. The last of the armored personnel carriers, mounted with .50 caliber machine guns, were rumbling through the streets. Mayor Loeb had just lifted a curfew that had been in effect from 7:00 p.m. to 5:00 a.m. That order allowed the jazz and blues clubs on Beale Street to reopen. But an eerie, uneasy calm hung over the city.

Despite the air of foreboding, King was back in the thick of the racial crisis in Memphis. He knew that his plan to stage a peaceful march posed great risks. If the federal court issued an injunction prohibiting him from marching in Memphis, King would face some tough questions. Would he disobey a court order and risk the consequences? Would another march, in defiance of the court, spiral into violence, further damaging his reputation? Would he be risking his life recklessly? He already feared for his personal safety, a fear heightened by the bomb threat to his flight that morning in Atlanta.

When he emerged into the airport terminal, four policemen in blue uniforms would be waiting for him at Gate 17. It was the detail under the command of Lieutenant Don Smith, with orders to protect King while he was in Memphis. King had not been notified in advance that there would be police security for him. He may have scarcely noted the presence of Smith and the three other officers with him. Police often were on hand to greet King when he was traveling. They were hardly worth a second glance.

Along with Smith's contingent, two African American police officers, Detective Edward Redditt and Patrolman Willie Richmond, were at Gate 17. They too were at the airport to watch King but for a different reason. Redditt and Richmond were wearing plain clothes. Their assignment was surveillance, not security. Their orders were to keep King "under continuous surveillance to see with whom he came in contact."[1]

Also in the greeting party for King was the Reverend James Lawson, pastor of the Centenary United Methodist Church in Memphis. Lawson, himself a notable civil rights leader, was hard to miss. He was wearing black horn-rimmed glasses and a white clerical collar under a black pleated shirt. After the garbage workers' strike began in Memphis, he had been chosen to head a support group known as the Community on the Move for Equality.

While waiting for King's plane to arrive, Lieutenant Smith talked to Lawson. Smith informed him that there would be police security for King in Memphis and asked about his schedule for the day. "We have not fully made up our minds," Lawson replied, according to a police report.[2] Smith would say later that he interpreted Lawson's response as evasive, that Lawson meant to sidestep the question. But Lawson would have another explanation. He would say that he had left the security issue for King to resolve. "That would be the way I would work," Lawson would say, years later. "I would not have worked independently of King for his security."[3]

Yet another face in the crowd at Gate 17 was Tarlese Matthews. An impassioned strike supporter, she had made a name for herself in local civil rights circles a decade earlier. She had demanded entry to the Memphis Zoo at Overton Park on a day other than Thursday. The zoo was open to blacks only on Thursdays (except when a Thursday coincided with a holiday, when only whites could attend). On non-holiday Thursdays a sign at the gate proclaimed: "NO WHITE PEOPLE ALLOWED IN THE ZOO TODAY." Stopped from entering one day when the zoo was closed to blacks, Matthews did not merely turn around and go home. She sued.

Her lawsuit forced the city to desegregate not just the zoo but also the nearby municipal park and golf course.

Matthews was at the airport in her gray-and-black Buick Electra to chauffeur King while he was in Memphis. She noted that Lieutenant George Davis, one of the officers in Smith's detail, was at the gate. She also recognized Detective Redditt nearby.

Matthews bristled. She knew that undercover police were monitoring the pro-strike meetings. She claimed that the police were intimidating the strikers, violating their rights to free speech and assembly, not enforcing the law impartially. She faulted the police for having employed what she regarded as brutal tactics during two pro-strike marches.

On February 23 the police had used clubs and the anti-riot agent Mace against the marchers. (How the incident started was a matter of dispute. Did a squad car crowd the marchers and run over a woman's foot, or did the marchers provoke the police by rocking a squad car?) On March 28, during the march led by King, the police had responded to the rioting by a small number of youths. Officers fired tear gas and once again clubbed many people who were protesting peacefully.

Matthews stopped Lieutenant Davis. "We have not invited any police," she said.[4]

Then she confronted Detective Redditt. He and Richmond had been working undercover as partners since the strike began. They had the delicate task—"snooping," the strike's supporters called it—of tracking pro-strike meetings, rallies, and marches and reporting their observations to the Inspectional Division of the Memphis Police Department.

Pointing a finger at Redditt, Matthews snapped, according to a police report, "I'm going to get you." The anger that she directed at Redditt reflected her deep distrust of the Memphis police, even of the African Americans on the force.

In the hallway beyond Gate 17, King paused before a knot of reporters. He invited questions. In its edition that morning the *Commercial Appeal* reported that Mayor Loeb probably would seek an injunction from US District Court judge Bailey Brown to bar King from marching in Memphis.

King was asked if he would obey such an injunction. "I have my legal advisors with me," he replied, "and conscience also has to be consulted." If the federal court in Memphis blocked him from leading the march, he said, it would amount to "a basic denial of First Amendment privileges. We stand on the First Amendment."[5]

If King violated a federal injunction, he would be scuttling a core principle of his longtime strategy. He had defied state court injunctions against SCLC demonstrations on the grounds that they were protected under the US Constitution. He had, however, never disobeyed a federal court injunction (although he had come close to doing so in Selma, Alabama). Favorable rulings of the federal judiciary had been a critical bulwark of the movement.

A reporter asked about the risk that people marching under King's banner might act violently during the upcoming protest, as they had on March 28. "We have been meeting with them," King said, interpreting the question to refer to a local Black Power group, the Invaders. "These groups have committed themselves to co-operation with us."

Another reporter asked a question that went beyond the immediate crisis in Memphis. He asked if the rioting during the march in Memphis six days earlier had caused King to rethink his plan for the Poor People's Campaign.

"Our plan in Washington is going on," King replied. "Memphis will not in any way curtail or deter it. We must spotlight the plight of the poor nationally."

What about NAACP president Roy Wilkins's comment that the Memphis rioting might be a preview of what lay ahead for the People's Campaign?

"He said that before," King shot back. "That's not new."

At the conclusion of the impromptu press conference King and his entourage of aides hurried down the glass-and-brick concourse toward the terminal exit. The four aides traveling with him were seasoned SCLC staff members. Ralph Abernathy, who was forty-two, was the oldest. The thirty-two-year-old Bernard Lee was the youngest. King himself was thirty-nine.

Abernathy had been at King's side, often literally, through the twelve tumultuous years bookended by the crises of Montgomery and Memphis. The two men were close. If anything should happen to King, he wanted Abernathy to assume the leadership of the SCLC.[6]

Andrew Young, the organization's executive vice president, was also close to King but played a different role. Abernathy was King's folksy sidekick. Young had the composure and polish of a diplomat, which in a sense he was. King would call on him to negotiate with hostile white politicians and businessmen.

Young and Dorothy Cotton, the SCLC director of education, had trained countless volunteers of all ages in the discipline of nonviolent protest. She was the lone woman in the SCLC's executive ranks. Bernard Lee, who looked a bit like King and dressed like him, was his frequent traveling companion.

Close behind them on the way to the airport exit was the four-man security detail under Inspector Smith. The four officers were not obvious choices to guard King. Two of them, Davis and Detective Ronald Howell ordinarily worked in vice and narcotics. The fourth, William Schultz, was on loan from homicide. All were white in a department still rife with racism two decades after the city broke the color barrier in hiring.

Memphis had no black police officers until 1948, when the first few were invited to join the department. But they did not have the same status as white officers. Blacks did not ride in patrol cars. They patrolled Beale Street and black neighborhoods on foot. They were not to arrest whites even if they witnessed a crime unfolding before their eyes. Years later, when the black officers were permitted to ride in patrol cars, they had to ride separately from whites.

By 1968, there were 100 blacks on the 850-man force. Even then, though, it was not uncommon for black officers to hear white colleagues say "nigger" on the police radio.[7] "Oh, a nigger was killed?" a patrolman's radio squawked loudly enough for King to hear during the violent outbreak of March 28.[8]

The two African American officers on the King watch, Redditt and Richmond, tagged along behind King, keeping a low profile. In 1966 Redditt had worked a security detail during King's visit to Memphis. He had shadowed King closely. King's down-to-earth manner had impressed him. "He had this warmth about him all the time," Redditt would recall years later.[9] Sitting with him one day at breakfast, Redditt asked what more it would take to further the civil rights movement. "Keep telling the folks the truth. They're going to wake up eventually," he remembered King saying.

Redditt looked different now. To work undercover during the garbage workers' strike, he had let his hair grow long in the Afro style, stowed his uniform, and donned khaki pants. In the crowd at the airport King might not have recognized Redditt.

King likely would have noticed Ernest Withers in the flock of people trailing him. The tall, ruggedly built Withers was a legendary African American photographer. On photo shoots throughout the Mississippi Delta, Withers had recorded images of Southern bigotry in all its naked ugliness. He combed the South for years, snapping photos of key civil rights moments for black-owned publications such as *Jet* magazine and the Memphis weekly *Tri-State Defender*. It was his classic shot that caught King on December 21, 1956, sitting at the front of a bus in Montgomery, Alabama. That triumphant day marked the end of the city's segregated bus system.

Now the forty-five-year-old Withers was covering King not entirely on his own account as a freelance photographer much admired in the movement. He was also moonlighting in the role of paid informant for the FBI, as the *Commercial Appeal* would report four decades later.

King exited the flat-topped, concrete-and-glass terminal on its upper departure level and climbed into the front passenger seat of Matthews's Buick. Abernathy, Young, and Lee sat in the backseat.

The Buick left the airport, heading toward the Lorraine Motel, a twenty-minute drive away. In a convoy close behind were cars carrying Withers, the undercover team of Redditt and Richmond, and Smith's four-man security detail.

Chapter 5

The Invitation

*There comes a time when one [must] take a position
that is neither safe nor politic nor popular.*

—MLK, sermon at the National Cathedral,
Washington, DC, March 31, 1968

KING FIRST HEARD in detail about the Memphis strike while he was attending a ministers' conference in Miami. He and dozens of other African
American clergy from around the country were at the Four Ambassadors
Hotel over the last weekend in February. Under the sponsorship of the
Ford Foundation they had gathered to discuss how to prevent the kind of
rioting that had convulsed the nation's inner cities. One of those attending
was Billy Kyles, pastor of the Monumental Baptist Church in Memphis.

Kyles, an old friend of King, was keeping a close watch on the developments surrounding the strike in Memphis. He was well aware too of the
Poor People's Campaign, which he knew was entering a critical phase and
absorbing King's energy almost to the breaking point. Mostly as a joke,
Kyles suggested to King that he add the strikers' cause to his heavy agenda.
"Man, we've got a garbage strike in Memphis," Kyles would remember
saying to King, "and we may have to get you to come in and help us out."[1]

By the third week of the walkout, the strikers felt that they had hit a
wall. It wasn't that Mayor Loeb was proving to be a tough negotiator. Until
the strikers returned to work he was refusing to negotiate—period. That
was a condition that the strikers rejected out of hand. To pressure Loeb to
reconsider, strike supporters asked national civil rights leaders Roy Wilkins

of the NAACP and Bayard Rustin, the chief organizer of the 1963 March on Washington, to come to Memphis and speak on their behalf. Wilkins and Rustin agreed. They spoke at a rally on March 14, but their appearance attracted little media coverage.

Kyles figured that King would make a much bigger splash and decided to invite King again to Memphis, this time not as a joke. He telephoned SCLC headquarters in Atlanta and left word. "When we first made the call," Kyles would recall, "he didn't get the message. The people who got the message said, 'You know we are really in sympathy with you guys, but we are so far behind on the Poor People's Campaign. We just don't have time to come to Memphis.'"[2]

At the same time, apart from Kyles's overture, Reverend Lawson was thinking about how King might help the strikers' cause. Lawson knew King well. He had conducted workshops in nonviolence for the SCLC and served on its board. As head of the community group supporting the strike in Memphis, Lawson now had something to ask of King in return. He called King to ask if he would come to Memphis and speak at a pro-strike rally.

In Lawson's retelling of the conversation King agreed right off to come to Memphis. Lawson would recall, "There was no hesitation. He was committed." Lawson would remember King as having said, "You're doing in Memphis what I want to do [with the Poor People's Campaign], namely, tie up this question of economic justice with racism."[3]

King figured that he could fit Memphis into his busy schedule with scarcely any downtime from the Poor People's Campaign. He would dash into the city and deliver a single speech. He would get up at four o'clock in the morning, catch a six o'clock plane to Memphis, speak at a rally for the strike and be in Washington for another event the same evening.[4]

Even the quick-hit scenario gave Andrew Young pause. He was perhaps King's most able adviser among the top-tier SCLC staff. He was smart, diligent, and reliable. Within three years of his joining the SCLC staff, in recognition of his obvious gifts as an administrator and strategist, King had named him executive director.

The two men were close in age. Young was just three years younger. They could relate openly and easily as contemporaries with similar backgrounds. Unlike Bevel, Jackson, Williams, and Abernathy, Young had not had to endure the hardships that typified the lives of many African Americans in the South. Like King, Young had grown up in a stable family—in Young's case, in New Orleans. His parents were well educated and financially comfortable. His father was a dentist, his mother a teacher. Theirs had been a solidly bourgeois life.

It seemed no coincidence that Young and King were fraternity men. Both had belonged to a prestigious black fraternity, Alpha Phi Alpha, King at Morehouse College, Young at Howard University.[5] Rather than pursue a career in dentistry, as his father would have liked, Young had chosen divinity school. He had worked in New York City for the National Council of Churches before joining the SCLC in 1961.

Despite the tight bond between them, King had not always followed Young's advice. Young's was the voice of caution. "I was constantly in the position of urging Martin to focus our limited staff resources and resist the temptation to respond to every worthy cause," he would explain years later.[6]

King came to value Young as a counterweight to the hotbloods on the SCLC staff. When they would demand that King plunge into some high-risk undertaking, Young would point out the pitfalls. From him King could count on hearing a careful, pragmatic argument. He was in effect a brake on the staff's passions, and they taunted him for it. He was their Uncle Tom, they would say. At times, even King could not resist ridiculing him with the same put-down.[7]

Young had implored King not to speak out against the Vietnam War. Better to keep his antiwar views to himself, Young had advised. Wouldn't it offend civil rights leaders who supported the war or believed that King's opposition to it would undercut progress on civil rights? Wouldn't denouncing President Johnson's war policy cost the movement a powerful ally in the White House?

King rebuffed Young's advice. (Young eventually would come around to agreeing with King's outspokenness on Vietnam.) When King felt deeply about his rightness on an issue, he could be headstrong and unyielding. Ben Hooks, a member of the SCLC board, shared Young's view on the question of Vietnam. Hooks, a judge and Baptist pastor in Memphis, was a devoted friend of King. At a board meeting, when the discussion turned to Vietnam, Hooks did not hold back. He would recall: "I asked the question, 'With Johnson doing all he could for civil rights, would it be better for us not to antagonize him at this point?' . . . When I made that statement, innocently, Martin ate me alive."[8]

As Young feared, King's declarations on Vietnam did offend some top civil rights leaders. Whitney Young, executive director of the National Urban League, objected to King mingling war policy and racial justice, which he said was doing a "disservice" to civil rights.[9]

And as Andrew Young and Ben Hooks had predicted, King's high-profile opposition to the Vietnam War had enraged Lyndon Johnson. The president had retaliated by turning a cold shoulder to King and the movement. Johnson had expected King to fall in line on Vietnam out of loyalty to him for his having maneuvered landmark civil rights legislation through Congress. "That goddamned nigger preacher," Johnson ranted privately about King.[10]

Now as King toyed with the idea of speaking to garbage workers in Memphis, Young felt another surge of misgivings. He doubted that King could duck into the crisis in Memphis, deliver a single speech, and then drop the strikers' cause like a hot potato.

As Young might have put it, King seemed to be forgetting the "lesson of Albany." In 1961 King had interceded in a desegregation campaign under way in Albany, Georgia. King had intended to appear once in a quick visit. He would lead a march in Albany and leave town. That would be it. But during the march, on December 14, he was swept up in a mass arrest of demonstrators and jailed. He found himself entangled in the Albany struggle. It became *his* campaign. He would be stuck in Albany for a year. It was the civil rights version of mission creep. The Albany campaign ended in futility when the city closed down its buses and other public facilities instead of desegregating them. As Dorothy Cotton would note, Albany proved that the SCLC, before starting a campaign, had to "send in a training team to prepare the community," organizing its supporters for massive, nonviolent protest.[11]

When Young thought about King's plan for a quick visit to Memphis, he saw the risk of another Albany in the making. He feared "that one speech would lead to two, and two would lead to his going to jail or something like that, because it was out of his control once he got involved."[12]

Then there was the urgency of the Poor People's Campaign. If King and his staff got mired in Memphis, as Young feared, it could delay the start of the Washington initiative. Young pointed out that, even if the campaign started on schedule, the time for pressuring lawmakers in the nation's capital would be short. Congress would adjourn as usual for its summer recess in late June or early July, certainly no later than the Fourth of July. As it was, Young told King, in that narrow window it would be hard to accomplish much."[13] Further delay would close the window all the more.

In sum, Young was dead set against King going to Memphis. He argued that the Poor People's Campaign ought to have the undivided attention of King and the staff. He pleaded with King not to go.

King was not persuaded. How could he ignore the compelling cause of Memphis, where the strike had developed into a major civil rights struggle? Perhaps no less important to him, Memphis offered a stage on which he could dramatize the antipoverty drive. How better to illustrate the face of poverty in the United States than to spotlight garbage workers, whose wages were so low that some were on welfare?

To Young's warning about the risk that King could become bogged down in Memphis, he replied, simply, "They just want me to come down and preach. And the Poor People's Campaign is about people just like this. And the least I can do is go down there."[14]

So King agreed to speak at a rally on March 18. A hectic speaking schedule that Monday had him hopscotching around the country. He flew from Los Angeles to New Orleans, then to Jackson, Mississippi, and finally to Memphis. He arrived in the Tennessee city for an evening speech. It was the thirty-fifth day of the strike.

The rally was at Mason Temple, the centerpiece of the six-building headquarters of the Church of God in Christ. The church, one of the largest African American denominations, with congregants worldwide, had been making its cavernous sanctuary available to the strike's supporters. Now they prayed that King's star power would fill Mason Temple.

Lawson figured that King's appearance at Mason Temple would draw a large crowd. He predicted a turnout of ten thousand. Sure enough, on the night of the rally, he watched as people arrived in droves. Then he headed to the airport to meet King's flight.

When King entered the terminal, Lawson apologized about the turnout at Mason Temple. "I'm sorry. I don't know what happened, but it doesn't look like you're going to speak to 10,000 people," Lawson said, according to an account by labor historian Michael Honey.

King's face fell. "Yeah, it looks, doctor, as though you might speak to 25,000 people," Lawson said. "He just lit up like a lantern," Lawson would recall.[15]

The eventual estimates of the crowd's size varied. Lawson would lower his to fifteen thousand. The police said the number was only nine thousand. Whatever the number, the crowd greatly exceeded the temple's capacity. As historian Joan Beifuss would decribe the scene, people were "sitting on steps, standing in aisles and doorways, spilling outside."[16] It was just past nine o'clock that evening when King entered the temple through a side door. Several striking workers escorted him to the podium.

Waiting to hear him was a boisterous throng. When they saw him on the podium, they leaped to their feet. Many raised their arms in clenched-fist salutes. A deafening, full-throated cheer filled the vastness of the sanctuary, seemingly rebounding from the steel girders overhead and suffusing King on the podium.

He was thrilled by the welcome. "He was surprised" Billy Kyles would say, "first of all to see the black community as close together as it was and having the old movement spirit. It really lifted him." The days when King could evoke such passion from a crowd fervently united behind him had seemed past. Suddenly that intensity was back. Kyles would remember how King fed on the crowd's exuberance, buoyed to hear them "whooping up everything he'd say."[17]

In his speech King portrayed the strikers' cause as right and just. "All labor has worth," he said. He extolled the Poor People's Campaign and linked the strike to that grand cause. He said that the garbage workers were "reminding the nation" that it was a "crime" for workers in "this rich nation" to receive "starvation" wages.

He implored the strikers to press on with their demands. To put clout behind the rhetoric, he called on the city's African American community to stay away from work and school for a day to pressure the mayor to accept the strikers' demands.[18]

As King neared the end of his speech, Lawson and Young conferred behind him on the speaker's rostrum. Lawson whispered to Young that King ought to return to Memphis and lead a march to bolster the strikers. Young scribbled a note to that effect and slipped it to King at the rostrum.

King glanced at the note but sat down without responding. Lawson and Young huddled with King. As though seized by a sudden force, he returned to the rostrum. In a strong, vibrant voice he proclaimed that Memphis could mark "the beginning of the Washington movement." If the strikers would like it, and of course they would, he announced that he would return to Memphis and lead them in a march to City Hall.

On an impulse he had committed himself more deeply into a tangled labor and racial dispute of a city in crisis. Abruptly, he had ditched his own plans and promised to come to Memphis a second time in support of the strike. As Beifuss would note, it was "an involvement that he had originally neither envisioned nor desired" when he had accepted the invitation to speak in Memphis.[19]

Chapter 6

The Mayor

I want you to stick it out so that you will
be able to make Mayor Loeb and others say yes,
even if they want to say no.

—MLK, speaking to Memphis
garbage workers, March 18, 1968

IF MEMPHIS WERE a thumbtack on a map of the United States, it would pin down a spot where the borders of Mississippi, Arkansas, and Tennessee converge. Memphis and the region surrounding it are commonly called the Mid-South. Memphis sees itself apart from both the Deep South and the Border States, like Kentucky to the north. Viewed through the lens of the Civil War, Memphis stands roughly halfway between Issaquena County in the Mississippi Delta (which once had the highest concentration of slaves anywhere in the United States) and the southernmost edge of Kentucky (a slave state until Lincoln's Emancipation Proclamation, though it never seceded from the Union).

King did not know Memphis well. Over the years he had breezed into the city for one purpose or another, a speech to a Baptist convention or a brief stopover en route to a nearby state. He was always, more or less, passing through.

The SCLC waged campaigns in many southern cities but steered clear of Memphis. Everyone knew that Memphis was a NAACP town. The Memphis chapter of the NAACP championed a civil rights agenda of its own under the leadership of accomplished African Americans. Prominent among them was lawyer, minister, and later judge Benjamin Hooks and Maxine Smith, who held a master's degree in French from Middlebury College in Vermont and who served as executive director of the NAACP in Memphis.

Unlike some other chapters of the NAACP, the one in Memphis did not turn to the SCLC for help—until 1968. As Andrew Young said years later, reflecting on the prevailing view at the SCLC toward Memphis: "They had it all together, and I said, 'They don't really need us.'"[1]

Memphis differed from southern cities like Little Rock and Birmingham in having navigated the turbulent years of racial tension during the late fifties and sixties without major strife until 1968. Yet in its racial profile it was undeniably deeply Southern. "Keep Memphis Down in Dixie" was the bumper-sticker slogan of a prominent mayoral campaign in the late fifties.[2]

A visitor to Memphis in 1968 need look no further for confirmation of the city's down-in-Dixie tradition than the prominent statue of Nathan Bedford Forrest, the Confederate cavalry general and first grand wizard of the Ku Klux Klan. The lofty statue of Forrest sitting erect in the saddle stood in a downtown park bearing his name. A plaque memorializing Forrest noted his "heroic raid to recapture Memphis from federal troops." What the plaque did not say was that he was one of the city's most successful slave traders in the years before the Civil War. The commerce at "Negro Mart" on Adams Avenue, where he dealt in slaves, was highly lucrative. One of his slaves could fetch as much as $1,000, a huge sum at the time.[3]

Once King accepted the invitation to support the strike in Memphis, he had much to learn about the city. It seems likely that he knew little about Henry Loeb, who had been mayor only three months. The perfect source for guidance about what made Loeb tick was Methodist minister Frank McRae. But King did not know McRae and was not in touch with him.

When the strike began in mid-February, Mayor Loeb turned to McRae as his confidant. The lanky, affable McRae and the mayor were old friends. During the crisis Loeb would invite McRae to the white-marbled city hall for lunch several times a week. Loeb would send out for hamburgers. The two men would eat in the mayor's office while two or three policemen in plain clothes stood vigil nearby. "He was so cheap he'd never buy anything but hamburgers, but I loved him," McRae would remember.[4]

Loeb's red-carpeted, wood-paneled office was spacious and handsomely appointed in a modern, manly style. The mayor sat in a high-backed leather chair at an oversize desk that seemed to magnify his bigger-than-life persona. Loeb, who stood six foot five, cut a strapping, square-jawed figure. "You knew damn well he was in the room when he was there," Joe Sweat, who was the city hall reporter for the *Commercial Appeal*, would recall years later.[5]

Loeb thought so highly of McRae that he asked him to officiate at his wedding and swear him in as mayor. Loeb was not a Methodist. Born a Jew, he had married an Episcopalian and in 1963 converted to his wife's faith. Loeb might have chosen an Episcopalian priest or a rabbi to marry him or swear him in. McRae presided at both ceremonies.

McRae was thirty-seven, ten years younger than the mayor, but they belonged to the same generation that came of age in the years before and during World War II. They grew up in a Memphis defined both by a high regard for courtly Southern manners and a rigid allegiance to white supremacy. When, decades later, McRae looked back at the Memphis of his youth, he spoke in fond superlatives. Memphis had been the cleanest, safest, quietest city in America, he would say.

The view of Memphis as an upright, exceedingly livable city was a general point of pride among its residents. It motto officially was the City of Good Abode.

It had not always lived up to its self-image. Before the Civil War, according to historian Joan Beifuss, it was "a brawling, muddy, Mississippi River town, jumping off place to the frontier Southwest."[6] Its mosquito-friendly swamps made the city an inviting host for yellow fever. During the 1870s, an epidemic of the mosquito-borne disease killed many thousands of residents and led to a mass exodus from the city.

The city flourished anyway. Its location as a favored port for paddle steamers plying the Mississippi advantaged its economy. It emerged, notably, as a bustling market for the trade in cotton. Its brokerages on Main Street handled not just cotton but also, as in the case of Nathan Bedford Forrest, slaves. Another leading slave trader, Wade Hampton Bolton, placed this ad in the *Memphis Appeal* in 1846: "I have for sale plenty of boys, men and women and some very fancy girls. I intend to have a constant supply through the season."[7]

The Memphis of McRae's youth was strictly segregated by race. He knew well the oddities and grotesqueries of Jim Crow life. There were water fountains for "whites," separate ones for "colored." Blacks had to sit in the back of buses even if there were no white passengers riding in them. Black women could shop for dresses in stores but couldn't try them on.

One Thursday in the late 1950s, a black chauffeur drove two grand dames from Greenville, Mississippi, to a special art exhibit at the Pink Palace art gallery in Overton Park. Upon their arrival the ladies discovered, to their dismay, that Thursday was "Negro Day" at the Pink Palace. Barred from entry, they returned to their car. All was not lost. They dispatched the chauffeur to enjoy the art exhibit in their stead.[8]

In 1967 McRae was named superintendent of the Methodist district for Memphis. He had a mandate from his bishop to address the poverty and other disadvantaged circumstances of the city's African American inhabitants. He took the assignment to heart. But when the sanitation workers' strike began the next year, McRae opposed it. He viewed it as an illegal, wildcat strike against the city. State law prohibited strikes by most public employees, including garbage collectors. McRae, moreover, was not aware of any grievance that would justify a step as extreme as a strike to shut down a service as vital to public health as garbage collection. Nor did McRae trust the garbage workers' union. Like many Memphians he was wary of organized labor.

McRae loyally sided with his good friend, the mayor. They had become acquainted through Loeb's wife, Mary. McRae had met Mary when they were students at Memphis State University, as the University of Memphis was then called. Mary, a stunning redhead, had been a Cotton Carnival queen. It was an honor reserved for attractive young women of high social standing. Her father owned large tracts of cotton-growing land in Arkansas and headed a large cotton brokerage in Memphis.

Loeb's marriage to Mary Gregg linked two of the city's wealthiest families. His family owned a large business, Loeb Laundry Cleaner Company. Its logo was conspicuous in brilliantly blue letters on its storefronts and the sides of the company's trucks that roamed city streets. Loeb may have been a homegrown Memphian, but he had attended elite schools in the East: Phillips Academy in Andover, Massachusetts, and Brown University in Providence, Rhode Island. Like John F. Kennedy, he had commanded a PT boat as a naval officer during World War II. On the wall of his mayoral office he proudly displayed a photo of a PT boat a quarter century after his navy days.

As reporter Sweat would remember, Loeb retained a sailor's command of "salty language, full of goddamns and son-of-a-bitches, and he enjoyed a good, bawdy story." But Loeb had an old-fashioned Southern manner in the company of women. Sweat would put it this way: "He had this gallant thing about women. If a lady was coming into his office, he'd put on a coat."[9]

After military service Loeb joined his father and brother in managing the family laundry business. His involvement in local civic affairs, including the Memphis Civitan Club and American Red Cross, kindled an interest in politics. In the early sixties, he launched a political career, first as public works commissioner, then mayor. As mayor from 1960 to 1964 he grudgingly complied with court orders to desegregate schools and other public facilities. But there was a limit to how much racial progress he was willing to accept. Rather than desegregate the municipal swimming pools, he simply closed them down.[10]

His father died in the mid-sixties, and Loeb quit city government to resume his work at the laundry. Not for long. In 1967 he plunged into a hotly contested mayoral race. His principal opponent was William Ingram, the incumbent mayor and, by comparison to Loeb, a racial moderate. Loeb presented himself as a "law and order" candidate. He had scant black support. He took office on January 1, 1968, under a restructured city government, in which a city council system replaced a five-member commission. The change resulted in three African Americans being elected to the council while vesting greater power in the mayor.

Just six weeks later, the garbage workers went on strike. As the strike took hold and garbage piled up throughout the city, the mayor reacted swiftly, sternly. He denounced the strike as illegal and demanded that the strikers return to work. "As a precondition to any rearrangement of wages and working conditions, the strike must end," he wrote in a letter to the workers that the *Commercial Appeal* published on February 29.

Loeb was adamant on another point. He maintained that under no circumstances would he yield on either of the strikers' central demands: recognition of their union as the workers' bargaining agent or introduction of a dues checkoff.

The support among whites for Loeb's tough stance seemed virtually unanimous. "Henry would go to the Rotary Club," McRae would later say, "and, man, they'd give him a standing ovation. And everywhere he went the people were applauding him."[11] King's embrace of the strike did not impress the white population. On the contrary, the prevailing view among them was that King was a menace, a radical troublemaker with communist leanings, who was inciting the city's blacks to violence.

As the mayor's friend and a community leader by virtue of his rank in the Methodist hierarchy, McRae had a close-up view of the strike. He came to see it as a transcendent racial conflict, and his and the mayor's views diverged. He began to question, in his words, the mayor's "bullheaded" position.

By mid-March, he was taking issue squarely with Loeb during their lunchtime chats. McRae recalled, "He wanted to live by the rules. I think he was hiding behind them somewhat." McRae would remember one day as particularly awkward: "I said, 'Henry, you're a compassionate person. This is wrong.' And Henry said, 'No, it's against the [Tennessee] law to strike against the municipality.' And I said, 'Henry, it doesn't matter.'"

That the mayor would invoke Tennessee labor law as his line in the sand seemed shortsighted and legalistic to McRae. It was a logic that McRae shared with King. As King would say in his speech at Mason Temple on March 18 defending the strike: "You are going beyond purely civil rights to questions of human rights."[12]

As the tensions in Memphis escalated, McRae became all the more alarmed. He tried to persuade Loeb that the situation was urgent. He would remember saying, "Henry, you're sitting on a powder keg. Please realize this."[13] But the mayor refused to yield to what he perceived as lawless intimidation.

Whites siding with Loeb saw King's speaking and marching in support of the strike as part of the lawless intimidation that might lead to violence. King's critics had a point when they accused him of deliberately provoking a violent reaction from Southern segregationists in elected office. That strategy had served him well in Birmingham. That city's public safety commissioner, Theophilus Eugene "Bull" Connor, had cracked down brutally against protesters in the name of maintaining public order. Police sicced snarling dogs on youths, and firemen blasted them with powerful hoses. The sheer horror displayed on TV screens had galvanized public support for the civil rights cause. (Afterward, in a White House meeting with King, President Kennedy quipped: "I don't think you should all be totally harsh on Bull Connor. After all, in his way, he has done a good deal for civil-rights legislation this year.")[14]

But Henry Loeb was no racist caricature, no Bull Connor. He behaved respectfully, graciously toward blacks and whites. As Sweat would say years later, "Every Thursday he had an open house, and black kids would come looking for a job. He would open the newspaper and pore over the classifieds with them."[15] When a firebombing left a black family homeless, the mayor offered an apartment to them rent-free.[16]

Fred Davis, an African American city councilor, would say about the mayor: "He was in many ways a racist, like other white folk at the time. But in a paternalistic sort of way, Loeb had a real concern for the workers. He considered them 'his men.' And he felt like the union was selling the men out for the dues checkoff."[17]

As Loeb saw it, even his refusal to recognize the garbage workers' union was protecting them from harm. He regarded the national union officials who were in town demanding the city's recognition of Local 1733 and a dues checkoff as paving the way to exploit the workers, and he would not allow it.

Loeb came to his anti-union bias naturally. His father broke a union that sought to organize workers at the Loeb laundry. Sweat would explain: "He grew up in a home where his father told him, 'If you can just keep the trucks rolling, you can break the back of a strike.'"[18] The Loebs' anti-union attitude was widely held in Memphis. According to historian Michael Honey, union organizers had to contend with racial division, court injunctions, and police violence in the city. Such impediments were "standard fare to break unions in Memphis."[19]

The mayor resolved to break the garbage workers' strike. King's return to Memphis on April 3 and the march he was planning for Monday, April 8, promised to inject new energy into the strike. Loeb was pursuing a counterforce: a federal injunction to stop King from marching.

A similar injunction had stymied King's campaigns in Albany, Georgia, in 1962, and Selma, Alabama, in 1965. In those cases King obeyed federal court orders that stopped him from leading marches. (In Selma he had turned marchers back halfway across the Edmund Pettus Bridge rather than proceed to Montgomery, as originally intended. Federal judge Frank Johnson ruled that King did not violate his injunction.)

If Loeb's hard line was breaking the strike, as seemed more likely each day, why should he settle on the union's terms? In the November mayoral election he had received only 2 percent of the black vote.[20] If he surrendered to the strikers' demands, he would offend the voters who had elected him. He would be yielding to coercion from the union, the black community, and Martin Luther King. In the view of many of his white constituents it would be a political betrayal.

The mail flooding into city hall was running one hundred to one in favor of his stand against the strike.[21] The city's two daily papers, the *Commercial Appeal* and *Memphis Press-Scimitar*, were stoutly behind him. "Memphis garbage strikers have turned an illegal walkout into anarchy and Mayor Henry Loeb is exactly right when he says, 'we can't submit to this sort of thing!'" the *Commercial Appeal* editorialized on February 23.

Not everything was going the mayor's way. Strike supporters were soon boycotting downtown stores. Sales were down, and merchants were pressuring Loeb to settle the strike. A few of Loeb's friends, especially Frank McRae, were whispering to him about the risk that racial tensions in the city could boil over into widespread civil unrest.

Chapter 7

Lorraine Check-In

Now that I want you to come back to
Memphis to help me, everyone is too busy.

—MLK, scolding his staff at a meeting
in Atlanta, March 30, 1968

IT'S A TWENTY-MINUTE DRIVE from the airport to the Lorraine Motel, where King was staying in Memphis. Arriving close behind the Buick that delivered King to the Lorraine was the police contingent: Inspector Smith's four-man security detail and the surveillance team of Redditt and Richmond. On Smith's orders three other officers—Inspector J. S. Gagliano and Lieutenants Jack Hamby and Joe Tucker—arrived at the Lorraine in another patrol car. They were at the motel "to assist in securing the area," as a police report would note.[1]

The Lorraine was a rare, if modest, example of urban renewal in a distressed area on the cusp of downtown Memphis. The motel, located at 450 Mulberry Street, looked spiffy next to the surrounding bars, pawnshops, and seedy warehouses located in the underbelly of Beale Street a half dozen blocks away.

The Lorraine had been a sixteen-room hotel that had fallen into disrepair until 1955, when Walter and Lorene Bailey bought it. In earlier years Walter had been a Pullman porter. After an attempt to run a turkey farm hit a dead end, the couple had entered the inn-keeping business. They started humbly, renting rooms out for seventy-five cents a night in a rooming house on nearby Vance Street.[2] Having acquired the forlorn, sixteen-room hotel, the

Baileys embarked on a plan for improving it. They spruced up the original building and added a freestanding, motel-style structure comprising almost fifty rooms, plus a swimming pool. They renamed the place for Lorene, tweaking the spelling. Motel ownership proved to be a good fit for Walter and Lorene, and they stuck to it.

The most noteworthy feature of the Lorraine was a sign that towered over the parking lot. In a medley of colors the sign seemed to declare that the motel deserved a certain regard. Crowning the top like a rooster's comb was a red arrowhead-shaped pointer indicating the entrance to the parking lot. Below was the name *Lorraine* in black script against a yellow background, followed by M-O-T-E-L, each fiery red letter set in a white circle. A massive, turquoise arch supported the whole edifice.

As a black-owned motel located near Beale Street, the Lorraine became known as *the* place to stay for African American visitors to the city. Among the notables who spent a night there during the Jim Crow era were music greats Ray Charles, Louis Armstrong, and B. B. King. In 1968 King could have opted for recently desegregated hotels, such as the posh Peabody downtown or the Holiday Inn Rivermont, which offered a spectacular view of the Mississippi River. He preferred the Lorraine.

He had stayed at the flat-roofed motel several times, often enough that the Baileys had designated Room 306 on the second floor as his whenever he desired it.[3] Though one of the motel's best, the room was not luxurious. There were two double beds, a rabbit-eared TV perched on a simple wooden dresser, two small table lamps, and a chair with striped upholstery. There was a basic bathroom accessible through a wide opening in a knotty-pine back wall.

When King arrived that Wednesday morning, Walter Bailey and his wife greeted him warmly. "Everywhere were smiles and handshakes," historian Joan Beifuss would write about the moment.[4] The Baileys always bent over backward to please King. The room rate was thirteen dollars a night, but they did not charge him. "We just felt a part of the Lorraine," Abernathy would say years later. "It is a black motel and, of course, they had a lot of catfish there, and Dr. King and I loved catfish, and they were not strict so far as room service [was] concerned."[5]

For all its appeal to King, the Lorraine posed a particular risk for anyone who might fear an assassin's bullet. There was no elevator. To reach Room 306, a guest had to climb one of two stairways and continue to rooms that opened onto a balcony. The stairways and balcony were nakedly exposed to Mulberry Street. Nothing except an iron railing sheltered the second-story balcony from the parking lot, which faced Mulberry.

The risk to King was obvious to Lieutenant Jerry Williams, an African American police officer on the Memphis force. During one of King's visits to the city Williams had warned him not to stay at the Lorraine "because of its exposed balconies," according to historian Michael Honey.[6]

If the warning stuck with King until April 1968, he did not heed it. Precautions did not interest him because he did not think anything or anybody could protect him against a determined assassin.

With King and almost the entire top echelon of his staff installed at the Lorraine, it became, in short order, the operational headquarters of the SCLC in Memphis. King and Abernathy checked into Room 306, which they were sharing. Andrew Young, Dorothy Cotton, and Bernard Lee fanned out to other rooms. Hosea Williams, Jesse Jackson, and James Orange turned up on Sunday. James Bevel had been in Memphis earlier that week before leaving for Chicago. He was expected back that night.

Also checked into the motel were members of the local Black Power group, the Invaders. They were hanging out at the Lorraine for ready access to King and his staff, with whom they were trying to cut a deal. The Invaders wanted money, financial support for a proposed "Liberation School" where they would teach black history and heighten pride in black identity.

They were not hard to spot. A dozen of them, including cofounders Charles Cabbage and John Burl Smith, were milling around the front door of the office that morning. Dressed in jeans, they wore their hair in Afros. Some wore dark glasses. Several sported amulets dangling from their necks.

Cabbage and Smith identified with the restless Black Power faction of the civil rights movement. In rhetoric, if not action, they rejected King's nonviolent approach. In the aftermath of the rioting on March 28, Cabbage stated his point of view in advance of King's return to Memphis. He told a newspaper reporter that whatever belief he might have had in nonviolent protest had "died" that day.[7] Presumably he was aggrieved by the aggressive police response to the riot.

Yet King, undeterred by the Invaders' Black Power rhetoric, intended to recruit them as parade marshals for the march he would lead on Monday. He regarded their cooperation as a key to a violence-free march. To secure the Invaders' cooperation, he was depending on his aides—especially Bevel, Williams, and Orange—to help win them over.

He would need his aides' cooperation. Securing their enthusiastic assistance in Memphis was testing his leadership. In Memphis, as elsewhere, King's charisma was the glue that bound the SCLC together. "We would argue like crazy," Dorothy Cotton would say of her fellow staff. "He would sit there quietly. When he spoke, we would shut up."[8] It was King who charted their course, mediated disputes, and built morale. Inducing his aides to pull in the same direction was not always easy. As Andrew Young would say, the staff "was a passionate group of wild men that sort of functioned like wild horses."[9] Dorothy Cotton would put it even more bluntly, terming the staff a bunch of "young, self-important egomaniacs."[10]

That the staff was headstrong and arrogant was hardly surprising. To join the SCLC staff meant forsaking, or at least delaying, a stable career and comfortable life. It meant running the risk of potential physical harm and possible death. No mild-mannered, submissive person was likely to enlist in the SCLC, and King was savvy enough to know it. He wanted young, ego-driven, risk-taking mavericks, and he had them. At times the infighting turned fierce. Only half-jokingly King and Abernathy "complained about the lack of nonviolence *within* SCLC," wrote historian Adam Fairclough.[11]

As he prepared to return to Memphis, King called an emergency meeting of his executive staff at Ebenezer Church on Saturday, April 30. "Memphis is the Washington campaign in miniature," he said, rallying his aides behind his audacious plan to stage another march in Tennessee.[12]

They replied with a barrage of objections. Young, fearing that exhaustion was impairing King's judgment, pointed to a lack of groundwork for a successful return to Memphis.[13] Bevel and Jackson were the most vehement. They denounced not only the Memphis plan but also the whole idea of the Poor People's Campaign. Bevel argued, instead, that the SCLC ought to devote all its energy to opposing the Vietnam War. "We don't need to be hanging around Washington," he barked. "We need to stop this war." Jackson termed the plan for Memphis "too small" and the one for Washington "too unformed," wrote historian Taylor Branch. Jackson demanded that King scrap the antipoverty crusade altogether. Jackson desired to replace it with Operation Breadbasket, his pet project in Chicago to improve the economic circumstances of African Americans.[14]

King's typical response to outbursts from his staff was to keep his cool. His manner was calm and Socratic. He would listen placidly while his aides fussed at one another or at him. All the while, in the words of historian Stephen Oates, he "would sit there thinking and scratching his whiskers. He would continue raising questions until they had worked through a problem collectively and reached a conclusion."[15]

But on this day he did not retain his usual composure and gentle authority. Unnerved by the setback in Memphis, he had no patience for his staff's carping and haggling. He erupted in rage. He ripped into Bevel and Jackson. He snapped first at Bevel: "You don't like to work on anything that isn't your idea." To Jackson he shouted, "If you want to carve out your own niche in society, go ahead. But for God's sake, don't bother me." King marched out of the meeting and left the staff to sort it all out. By the end of the meeting, which dragged on for six hours, the staff swallowed their objections. King was their leader, and they would follow him to Memphis.[16]

Dorothy Cotton would remember the tenor of the meeting: "There was a lot of energy. Everybody just arguing and expressing their opinions. But it was clear. We were going to go. When Martin spoke, it was, like, the discussion was over."[17] Abernathy would tell Coretta King, "We are all together now. We are going to Washington by way of Memphis."[18]

They were all together in acceding to King's desire that they go to Memphis. But they were not all together in their desire to go. Tensions between King and the staff were following them to Tennessee. Once he arrived, Jackson called his wife, Jackie, to report that the staff was "not supportive" of King. "They're rumbling," Jackson told his wife. "They don't want to be here, but we're stuck."[19]

King must have sensed that he had not seen the end of Bevel and Jackson's nettlesome challenge to his leadership. He trusted that they would fall in line behind him in Memphis anyway. Headstrong and defiant, verging on insubordination, they offered something that King's other aides did not. They were young, hip, and brash. Bevel was thirty-one; Jackson, twenty-six. The gap in years was not that large—King was eight years older than Bevel, thirteen years older than Jackson—yet in movement terms they were separated by a generational chasm.

Bevel and Jackson had come of age in the movement as undergraduate seminary students in the early sixties. They were in the forefront of a more aggressively defiant style of protest. They had been among the first to put their bodies on the line in sit-ins, nonviolent but unyielding, at segregated lunch counters. They had been cursed, beaten, and spit upon, and the experience had toughened them. Theirs was a confidence, a swagger, born of youthful courage.

They did not conform to the tacit SCLC executive dress code of muted dark suits and staid ties. Bearded and gaunt, Bevel dressed in denim overalls, a skullcap over his shaved head. The boyishly handsome Jackson, who had been a football star at North Carolina A&T, often wore jeans, the cuffs turned up high above the ankles.

They could relate more easily to the restless, angry generation of young African Americans, whose allegiance King was eager to earn. Bevel and Jackson might be headache-provoking, but he needed them. What's more, he had other more pressing matters on his mind than smoothing out relations with Bevel and Jackson.

Chapter 8

Damage Control

If we don't have a peaceful march in Memphis,
no Washington. No Memphis, no Washington.

—MLK, quoted by Jim Lawson

KING HAD NO TIME TO LOSE. He had five days to drum up support, recruit and train marshals in the discipline of peaceful protest, and pursue all possible means to preclude another violent outburst during the march on April 8. He was expecting thousands of participants. Not only garbage workers would march. He was urging students to skip classes at high schools and colleges and march with him. There were reports that thousands of people from out of town would converge on Memphis to join the march.

King was counting not only on his staff for organizational support. He was also expecting African American leaders in Memphis to bolster his efforts. He had to identify the religious and political figures with the most influence in the community, and recruit them to the cause. It was not unlike organizing an electoral campaign for public office except for one inescapable fact. He had little time to pull it off. The march was set for Monday, five days away.

He would be bucking the mayor's fierce resistance and the contempt of most white Memphians. David Caywood, a white lawyer who closely monitored the events surrounding King in 1968, would say, years later, that many whites abhorred King. "He was the lightning rod for all the segregationist attitudes here in Memphis," noted Caywood.[1]

Nor were the major Memphis newspapers welcoming. In its morning edition of April 3, the *Commercial Appeal* previewed King's return to the city that day with an editorial headlined "Take the March to Court." The paper decried King's plan to lead another march in Memphis. It called for federal marshals and endorsed the mayor's expected attempt to secure an injunction barring King from marching. "There is no reason," the editorial said, "why Memphis should have to take a second chance of downtown rioting just to allow Dr. King to wipe out the stain left by his previous 'nonviolent demonstration.'"

The usually milder afternoon paper, the *Memphis Press-Scimitar*, ran a barbed editorial of its own that day. It quoted NAACP leader Roy Wilkins expressing doubt that King could prevent violent outbursts during the Poor People's Campaign. The *Press-Scimitar* likewise said that King was courting violence by staging a second march in Memphis. Applying Wilkins's critique to King's upcoming march, the paper editorialized: "All good, practical advice for any mischief-maker, black or white."

If King had much to learn about Memphis, he would have been familiar with its basic contours. It was, after all, another southern city. Its DNA did not differ all that much from what he knew from his deep experience living and working in other southern cities. Further, he had friends in Memphis, including Baptist preachers Ben Hooks and Billy Kyles, to whom he could look for advice. In 1959 King had come to Memphis to campaign for two African American candidates, Hooks for juvenile court judge and Russell Sugarmon for public works commissioner. But Memphis was not Atlanta or Montgomery, cities he knew intimately. It was not terrain that he knew well. Much could go wrong.

A first order of business now that he was back in Memphis was connecting with local preachers. At 12:05 p.m. he departed the Lorraine in Tarlese Matthews's Buick for a meeting at Centenary Church. It was a redbrick building with white trim, unremarkable except for its long, sharply pitched roof. The Buick halted in front of the church, followed by two squad cars carrying Smith's four-man detail. Also arriving on the scene, in an unmarked car, was the two-man surveillance team of Redditt and Richmond.

Smith's detail promptly "secured" the front and rear entrances to the church, as a police field report would note.[2] During the two hours that King remained inside the church, Smith and his men stayed in their cars.[3] Redditt and Richmond, however, departed quickly. On orders from headquarters, they drove to a fire station on South Main Street near the Lorraine to set up a surveillance post. To camouflage their presence, they papered over a back window of the fire station, leaving a small peephole. The window offered a view of the Lorraine across Mulberry Street.

King entered the church along with aides Abernathy, Young, and Jackson. Waiting inside were Lawson, the Centenary pastor, and about thirty other black clergymen. Their clout as strike supporters was hard to overestimate in the religiously devout African American community of Memphis. At Sunday services they were blessing the strike, appealing to their congregants for support, and soliciting donations. They raised many thousands of dollars for the union's strike fund, which was helping to keep food on the strikers' tables.

The meeting at Centenary was in the church's Fellowship Hall, a barren room equipped with little more than folding chairs. King rose to address the clergy. The fallout over the riot on March 28 still hung darkly in the air. King wanted to dispel the cloud of despair. Speaking quietly, he reminded the ministers that he was in Memphis to lead a nonviolent march. He called on them to close ranks behind him, saying that unity was crucial. There would be no violent disruption of the march this time, he assured them.[4]

King reminded the ministers that it was a smattering of youths, not garbage workers, who had caused the trouble six days earlier. King denied that the garbage workers were in any way at fault for the violence.[5] Without out excusing the rioters, King sought to relate their criminality to poverty. According to an informant's account of the meeting as relayed to the FBI, King said that the youths who had smashed windows and looted stores were "actually to be pitied for all they have ever known is poverty and the economic war attendant on living in poverty."

King went on to say that the ministers should not lose sight of what the struggle in Memphis was all about. On one basic level it was a labor dispute. It was, he said, about raising the wages and improving the working conditions of the garbage workers. That was the goal.

Then he called on Jesse Jackson to speak. Jackson, in charge of the SCLC's Operation Breadbasket in Chicago, proposed an economic boycott in Memphis to mirror what he was doing in Chicago. There would be an appeal to strike supporters not to buy the products of big corporations, such as Coca-Cola or Wonder Bread—the kind of markets where blacks had consumer power. Jackson said the economic boycott would translate into political pressure because the corporations would insist that the mayor settle the strike.[6]

While Jackson was talking, King headed to Lawson's pastoral office to speak with two local lawyers, Louis Lucas and Walter Bailey. They had been in federal court that morning to oppose the city's petition for an injunction against King. Lucas and Bailey had rushed from the courthouse to brief King. The news was not good. At a hearing before Judge Bailey Brown, the city's lawyers had asked for an injunction on the grounds that it was crucial to prevent another riot. They had argued that King's march through the tense city likely would "cause great hazard, danger and irreparable harm." The judge had acted swiftly, granting a temporary injunction. It prohibited King, Abernathy, Williams, Bevel, Orange, and Lee from "organizing or leading a parade or march in the City of Memphis" over the next ten days.[7]

At Centenary Church, Lucas and Bailey told King that he could expect a federal marshal to serve his aides and him with a copy of Brown's order that day. In fact, they said, the marshal was expected to appear at the church momentarily.

For days King had been bracing for the possibility of an injunction. He had discussed the matter with Jim Lawson by phone over the weekend. As he plunged into the crisis in Memphis, King was turning to the Methodist minister as a sounding board. King had a high opinion of Lawson, as he would say publicly at a pro-strike rally that night. King would hail him as a longtime fighter for the rights of African Americans.[8]

King and Lawson had bonded the first time they met, in February 1957. Lawson was studying for a master's degree in theology at Oberlin College in Ohio. King was on campus to speak. They were the same age, then both twenty-eight, Lawson just four months older. Both were the sons of preachers. A pacifist, Lawson later refused induction into the army during the Korean War and served thirteen months in federal prison.

Lawson had looked into Gandhi's concept of nonviolent protest and adopted it as his own. He developed a sense of rectitude and fierce resolve to push the limits of nonviolent civil disobedience. In the late 1950s, as a PhD divinity student at Vanderbilt University, Lawson was in the forefront of the sit-in movement, leading students to desegregate the lunch counters of department stores in Nashville. Vanderbilt expelled him.

Lawson landed at Centenary as its pastor in 1962 and was soon deeply immersed in civil rights protest in Memphis. He quickly adopted a confrontational approach. He told a reporter, as quoted in the *Commercial Appeal* on November 30 of that year, "Negroes who seek improvements in education, income and housing can probably best realize their goals through massive social dislocation." If the demands were not met, Lawson threatened to make "it impossible for government to operate." He did not wait for a court order to integrate the city's restaurants. He and his wife, Dorothy, and their young son, John, simply showed up at a whites-only cafeteria and stood in line for food. They were served.[9]

If Lawson appeared more righteously pure than King, he did not possess the same warmth and affability. People complained that Lawson was holier-than-thou and off-putting. "He was not palatable," remembered Frank McRae, the superintendent of the Memphis district of the Methodist Church that oversaw Lawson's pastorate at Centenary. "He was not well received in the white community, because Jim had this rough veneer. His whole strategy was confrontational."[10]

Lawson was exhibiting that steely resolve in advising King to fight a court injunction that might stop him from marching in Memphis. Lawson would recount what he told King: "So I had called him as soon as I could and told him that I was preparing to organize against it. We'd get lawyers."[11] If Judge Brown did not lift his injunction before the march on Monday, Lawson urged King to defy the order.

In 1963, circuit court Judge W. A. Jenkins had enjoined King from demonstrating in Birmingham. King had led protesters into the streets of Birmingham anyhow. He was arrested and thrown in jail. But Jenkins was a judge of an Alabama state court. This time, in Memphis, the stakes were much higher. King was not dealing with the Tennessee equivalent of Jenkins's edict under Alabama state law—an order flagrantly tainted by segregationist bias. If he defied Brown's injunction, he would be rebuking the authority of a federal, not a state, judge.

Andrew Young would recall, years later, that federal judges were "our best ally, and we didn't want to run against them."[12] Ralph Abernathy, also commenting years later, would put the point even more strongly: "After all, we had made obedience to federal courts a central argument in our efforts to desegregate the South."[13]

A string of cases crucial to civil rights progress had included two decided by the US Supreme Court: one in 1954, *Brown v. Board of Education*, banned the racial segregation of public schools, and another, two years later,

Browder v. Gayle, invalidated the segregated bus system of Montgomery, Alabama. To violate Brown's order would cross a divide with potentially grave consequences. It might impair King's reputation with the federal judiciary and cost the movement a critical ally.

When considering how to respond to injunctions against him in earlier crises, King had consulted Ben Hooks. He was perhaps King's closest friend in Memphis. As a young student he had excelled in the city's segregated public schools before going on to Howard University in Washington, DC, and the DePaul University College of Law in Chicago. He had come home to practice as one of the first African American lawyers in Memphis. He split his time between the law and a job as pastor of the Middle Baptist Church. In 1965 he was appointed a criminal court judge, the first African American in that post in Memphis.

King had often turned to Hooks as a trusted adviser. He had recruited him for the SCLC board and relied on him to oversee its books and order its finances. But as he pondered what to do about Judge Brown's injunction, King did not seek Hooks's counsel. There was no need, because King knew what he intended to do. According to Hooks, King had decided, "if the judge said no, he was going to march anyway, knowing that the police would break it up and he'd be collared immediately to jail."[14] King, apparently, had concluded that the imperative to march in Memphis outweighed the potential hostility from the federal bench should he defy Brown's injunction.

After lawyers Lucas and Bailey briefed King, he asked Lawson once again how he ought to respond to the injunction if it remained in effect on the day of the march. Lawson reiterated his advice: King ought to march no matter what.[15]

King waited awhile in Lawson's office for the federal marshal to arrive and serve Brown's order. But there was an inexplicable delay. Having skipped breakfast in the rush to the Atlanta airport that morning, King was famished. He departed Centenary, leaving word that the marshal could find him at the Lorraine.

Chapter 9

The Injunction

*The federal courts have given us
our greatest victories, and I cannot, in good
conscience, declare war on them.*

—MLK, announcing that he would obey a federal
injunction, Albany, Georgia, July 20, 1962

IT WAS ALMOST 2:30 that Wednesday afternoon before King arrived
back at the Lorraine. Smith and his three officers, still close behind, secured the area around the motel.[1]

King headed to the second-floor dining room of the Lorraine to order
lunch. He was eating at 2:50 when US marshal Cato Ellis pulled his car
into the motel parking lot. King did not wait for Ellis to find him, but
bounded downstairs right away to greet him. Ralph Abernathy, Andrew
Young, Bernard Lee, and James Orange followed on King's heels to confront Ellis and a photographer from the *Memphis Press-Scimitar* in the
parking lot.

The photographer's photo published in the paper would show the tall,
bespectacled Ellis standing in the motel's parking lot, tendering a sheaf
of papers toward King and the four aides. Even at arm's length they likely
could have seen the heading on the cover page: *City of Memphis v. Martin
Luther King, Jr., et al.* Later, when they sat down to read the full text, they
would see these opening words: "It appearing to the Court that it is proper
that a temporary order should issue herein."

Underlying Judge Brown's order was an unstated but unmistakable threat. If King and his aides did not abide by the judge's ruling and marched in Memphis anyway, they would likely be jailed for contempt of court. It all added up to the threat of a roadblock standing in the way of the planned march on Monday.

Yet, oddly, the photo shows King and his aides grinning at the stern-faced Ellis. Dealing with court injunctions was then almost a routine, though nonetheless galling, matter for King. His spirits lifted by food in the belly, he apparently had cracked a joke to put his aides at ease. They did not seem to be showing disrespect for Ellis but rather were breaking the tension of the moment with a bit of levity.

The injunction in hand, King climbed the stairs to the second floor of the Lorraine and entered Room 307. Abernathy, Young, Lee, and Orange filed into the room behind him. A team of lawyers led by Lucius Burch was waiting. With Burch were three young associates from his firm. Also in the room were Lucas and Bailey, the two lawyers who had represented King in federal court the day before. A few local ministers also squeezed into the room.

Two beds occupied much of the space. King sat on the inner edge of one bed. Burch sat on the other so that they faced each other. King's aides and Burch's associates perched on the outer sides of the beds, their knees almost touching, or sprawled on the floor. Abernathy was sitting apart, still scooping the last of his fried-chicken dinner off a paper plate.

Burch was widely regarded as one of the best trial lawyers in Memphis if not the best. He was fifty-six years old, solidly built, with a broad, handsome face, receding hairline, and barrel chest. He was known as having a steel-trap mind enhanced by a virtually photographic memory. His fellow litigators of the Memphis bar held him in high regard bordering on reverence. In a hearing on the injunction the next day, James Manire, the lead lawyer for the city, would pay homage to him, even though they were on opposite sides of the case.

Addressing Judge Brown, Manire said, "I always get sort of attracted by Mr. Burch."

Judge Brown interjected, "Maybe you are mesmerized, Mr. Manire?"

"I am," Manire replied.[2]

The day before, an urgent call from the American Civil Liberties Union had drawn Burch into the case. The ACLU legal director in New York,

Mel Wulf, had heard about the injunction issued against King. He called J. Michael Cody, who was a thirty-two-year-old associate in Burch's firm and an ACLU board member. Wulf told him, as Cody would recount: "We don't want it to happen that King marches without the injunction being lifted because we're depending on federal injunctions to help the movement. You know, they have been the backbone of the movement."[3]

Figuring that King ought to have a seasoned trial lawyer representing him, Cody turned to Burch. His full name was Lucius Edward Burch Jr. The scion of a wealthy Tennessee family, he grew up on a large farm outside Nashville and attended Vanderbilt University, where his father was dean of the medical school. His grandfather had been a secretary of the US Senate and, as Burch would openly and ruefully admit, a slaveholder. Among Burch's ancestors were two of the three Tennesseans who had occupied the White House, Andrew Jackson and James K. Polk.[4] (The third was Andrew Johnson.)

As a young man, Burch had a zest for pranks and a yen for adventure. While a student at Vanderbilt Law School, he caught some fish and kept them alive and swimming by storing them in a drinking water tank near the office of the law school's dean. At his brother's wedding, he displayed a shotgun as though to suggest that it was a shotgun wedding. It wasn't.[5] Other stories had him shooting clay pigeons with Ernest Hemingway in Cuba, hunting game for bounty in Alaska, and living on a sailboat in Siberia.[6]

Burch had a defiant, contrarian streak. He seemed born to challenge arrogance and power. "He always didn't like somebody who would tell him what he had to do," Cody would say of him years later.[7] Burch was a thorn in the side of E. H. Crump, the city's longtime political boss. As Crump's electoral machine shifted into high gear to promote its slate of candidates, Burch advocated against them. His views were progressive, yet he straddled the divergent worlds of liberal politics and conservative highbrow society. Even while championing civil rights, he belonged to two of the city's most privileged and exclusive playgrounds, the Memphis Country Club and the Hunt and Polo Club.

Burch took it upon himself to tear down the wall that excluded black lawyers from the Memphis Bar Association. He plotted with local civil rights leaders to maneuver the Memphis establishment into desegregating the municipal library and other public facilities.

But when he was asked to represent King, Burch hesitated. His firm's clientele consisted of blue-chip corporations like the Standard Oil Company and the Illinois Central Railroad. Having King as a client "was not the sort of thing they like to see their lawyer engaged in," Burch would say later.[8] Knowing that many Memphians loathed King, Burch ran another risk if he advocated on his behalf. "You've got to expect," Burch would note, "there might be somebody that comes onto the panel [in a jury trial] and says, 'Well, there's the goddamn son-of-a-bitch that represented Martin Luther King! That nigger-lover. I'll fix him.'"[9]

Before agreeing to represent King, Burch insisted on meeting him, sizing him up face to face. He had questions, doubts that he wanted to put to rest. Was King a reasonable man? Did he really believe in the nonviolence that he espoused? What did he intend to achieve by returning to Memphis? How did Memphis fit into his overall, national strategy at the time?

Now in Room 307 at the Lorraine, Burch took charge. As Walter Bailey would recall, Burch said, at once, "Dr. King, I'm going to get right to the point." He asked: would King like Burch to represent him? If so, Burch proposed petitioning Judge Brown to lift the pending injunction. King confirmed that indeed he desired Burch to proceed in that manner.

Burch went on, "Now I want to ask a few questions and find out a few things."[10] He asked about King's view of the rioting on March 28. It had been a "complete fiasco," King replied, saying that it resulted from "poor planning."

In the aftermath of the riot, King went on, he believed that his whole future and, in particular, the Poor People's Campaign, "depended on his being able to have a nonviolent march in Memphis."[11] King said he was under attack from black militants who rejected his approach. To counter the militants, King told Burch, he had to prove in Memphis that nonviolence still worked.[12]

Burch asked, obliquely, if King would obey the injunction should Judge Brown refuse to vacate his order. King said he would march in any event, even if he had to disobey a court injunction.[13]

King knew that he would be on weaker legal ground in defying a federal injunction, in comparison with a state injunction. In state court he had disputed segregationist laws as violating his rights under the US Constitution. If King defied an order that the federal judiciary deemed lawful under the Constitution, he might have to fall back on his personal concept of unjust law as his only defense. He had touched on the concept in his famed "Letter from Birmingham City Jail": "An unjust law is a code that is out of harmony with the moral law ... that is not rooted in eternal law and natural law."[14] That is, King was saying that on his own authority he could decide which laws were just or unjust under natural law.

Justifying civil disobedience on the basis of natural law posed a problem for King because it endorsed a principle on which others might act in ways he regarded as objectionable. Why couldn't a man who was a segregationist, for example, contend that *his* concept of natural law justified disobeying court orders that mixed the races in schools or in marriage?

Burch suggested a strategy that might rescue King from the dilemma of either obeying a federal injunction or defying it on the legally flimsy basis of a natural law defense. He told King to expect that Judge Brown probably would not lift his order without insisting on some restrictions to minimize the chance that the march might turn violent. Burch said that if King would agree to abide by restrictions that would minimize the risk of violence, the judge might allow the march to go forward. Yes, King told Burch, he would accept such terms.

Burch would say later of King, "He completely reassured me that [his intention] was not phony in any degree and that it was just exactly what it was represented to be, the right of these people to express by assembly, petition, and demonstration what they felt was a just grievance."[15] King did not appear to be phony or deceptive at all. Rather, Burch remembered him as plainspoken and straightforward.

Someone asked King which group he feared more, white racists or Black Power militants. David Caywood, one of the young associates with Burch, recalled King responding that it "could easily be either group, but that wasn't the issue. The issue was to do whatever was necessary to make the [march] safe."[16] Thus reassured, Burch had no second thoughts about representing King. He would earn no fee. He was taking the case pro bono.

Looking back on the Burch-King meeting, Cody would recall the hushed atmosphere in the room. Except for Burch and King, almost nobody uttered a word. Cody knew the story about Burch's skeet-shooting adventure with Hemingway. As the story had it, Burch had not been intimidated by the fame of the legendary writer or by his overbearing personality. He had refused to "play second fiddle" to Papa Hemingway, Cody said.[17]

In the presence of King, however, Burch showed a surprising humility. It was a rare instance of Burch deferring to someone, Cody would say. He attributed Burch's reaction to a kind of spell cast by King's harmonious voice and calm manner. It was as if King possessed "an almost messianic or historical aura," Cody would say.[18]

That afternoon Burch and the city's lawyers met with Judge Brown in his chambers at the courthouse. Brown agreed to schedule a re-hearing on the injunction at 9:30 the next morning. Returning to their genteel law office off Court Square in downtown Memphis, Burch and his associates prepared to work all night building a case against the injunction.

Chapter 10

Invaders

We must forever conduct our struggle on the high plane of dignity and discipline. We must not allow our creative protest to degenerate into physical violence.

—MLK, "I Have a Dream" speech, August 28, 1963

THE FEDERAL INJUNCTION threatened to derail the march on Monday, but that was not King's only worry. If he did lead the march, with or without the court's blessing, there was the alarming possibility that rowdies would replay the violence of March 28.

King was pursuing a strategy to avoid that outcome. He intended to recruit the Invaders as parade marshals. He reasoned that if the Black Power group marched under his banner, younger and more disaffected members in the African American community would take their cues from the Invaders and not cause trouble during the march.

King believed that a similar strategy had worked for him in Chicago in 1966, when he had been pursuing a campaign to improve the deplorable state of the city's slum housing. To build grassroots support, he sought the cooperation of ghetto residents. Recruiting large numbers of them to put their bodies on the line in marches and protests became an overriding goal. But his efforts to mobilize support in the slums stalled without the involvement of an inner-city power broker: the street gangs of Chicago.

So King met with the gangs—the Vice Lords, Cobras, and Blackstone Rangers—seeking their support. It did not go well. He was stunned by their belligerence, their angry tirades, and coarse language. All the same, King did not stop talking with them. The sessions stretched late into many a night. He tried reasoning with them in a kind of tutorial, pointing out why they should trust him, why they should cooperate with him, why they ought to believe in nonviolence. Historian Stephen Oates described the tenor of the talkathons: "Gently, with great sincerity, King would explain the nature and purpose of nonviolence, asking them to try it as an experiment and put away their guns and knives."[1]

Against all odds, his words struck a responsive chord with some gang members. According to one estimate, two hundred of them pledged themselves to nonviolent marches following King through the streets of Chicago. From the experience of Chicago he drew a lesson. As he wrote in his 1967 book, *The Trumpet of Conscience*, "I am convinced that even very violent temperaments can be channeled through nonviolent discipline."[2]

What worked in Chicago, he concluded, could serve as a model for defusing the Black Power militancy that he feared might disrupt the Washington campaign. At a news conference on February 16, 1968, he had unveiled details of the antipoverty push. On the question of how he would counter Black Power–inspired violence, he cited his success with the gangs in Chicago. "We've worked in communities before where nationalists existed, where persons who believe in violence have existed," he said, "and yet we've been able to discipline them." He cited his experience with the Blackstone Rangers, terming them "the worst gang in Chicago," but said they had "marched in the demonstrations with us, and they never retaliated with a single act of violence."[3]

In Memphis the Invaders were eager to talk to King. About a dozen of them were checked into Rooms 315 and 316 of the Lorraine. That morning they had met with King's aides. Next they were to meet with him. Early in the afternoon, Charles Cabbage led his group to the dining room on the second floor of the motel to wait for him.

It would not be the first time that King had met with Cabbage. He and two other Invaders had turned up at King's room in the Holiday Inn Rivermont on the morning after the riot. (When the rioting broke out, King had taken refuge at the Holiday Inn in accord with a policeman's instructions. The officer had warned that the mayhem in the streets would block the route to the Lorraine, and he had escorted King to the Holiday Inn, where he stayed the night.)

According to one unofficial report that circulated immediately after the riot, it was the Invaders who were responsible for the looting and vandalism or at least had provoked youths to violence. King was aware of the report and believed it to be true. His despair over the rioting had not eased. He was profoundly depressed. Even so, he greeted Cabbage and his companions courteously. King wanted to know: would the Invaders help him stage a peaceful march?

Cabbage would remember how much at ease he felt in King's company. He would say that he could feel "peace around that man. It was one of the few times in my life when I wasn't actually fighting something."[4] In just a few moments, it seemed that they had a deal. The Invaders would have a voice in planning the march. In exchange, King would help them secure funds to support their community-outreach programs in the inner city.

To nail down the agreement, King had assigned James Orange, Hosea Williams, and James Bevel to continue the discussions with the Invaders. On the evening of April 1, the Invaders and aides had gathered at the Lorraine.

Facing off against the trio of Orange, Williams, and Bevel required a certain daring. All three were hardened paladins of the civil rights struggle. Orange, a giant of a man, had been on the receiving end of police assaults during SCLC demonstrations in Birmingham. Williams, a heavily bearded Korean War veteran, had been savagely beaten at a bus station for drinking from a water fountain for whites only. He had been in the thick of the SCLC campaign in St. Augustine, Florida, and had been teargassed and beaten horribly during the storied voting-rights march at Selma, Alabama. According to Dorothy Cotton, he especially among the SCLC staff had the chops to deal with "street dudes."[5] Bevel, a fast-talking ordained Baptist pastor, had shown his fearlessness facing vicious mobs during protests to desegregate lunch counters in Nashville and at bus stops during the 1961 Freedom Rides. He was on the front lines during protests in Birmingham, Selma, and Chicago.

If Orange, Williams, and Bevel presented a formidable front, they would nonetheless meet stubborn resistance from the Invaders. From the outset of the negotiations Cabbage and his group had relentlessly demanded money from the SCLC—lots of it. The talks had continued late into Monday night. By the end of the jawboning marathon Orange had all but pledged that the SCLC would satisfy the Invaders' demands. But he cautioned: the final say would be up to King.

Cabbage, John Burl Smith, and the third Invaders cofounder, Coby Smith (no relation to John Burl), were part of a young, restless, disaffected generation of African Americans for whom the siren of Black Power resonated powerfully. In 1968, Cabbage was twenty-three, Coby Smith a year younger. Racial bigotry had shaped their early years. As a child in Memphis, Coby Smith had no illusions about the second-class status of African Americans. He would remember: "They used to have an old saying when I was a kid, 'Dogs that chase cars and niggers that chase white women do not last long.'"[6]

Blacks of Smith and Cabbage's generation, however, had seen some racial barriers fall. Emboldened by the progress, they were impatiently demanding the removal of those that remained. Not coincidentally, their generation of blacks was developing a growing sense of self-worth and empowerment. Nothing summed it up better than James Brown's song, "Say It Loud—I'm Black and I'm Proud," that rocketed to the hit parade after its release in 1968.

Cabbage and Coby Smith had been standouts at Memphis's all-black schools. Cabbage had starred on the football and basketball teams at Carver High. Smith had been the student body president at Manassas High. He was one of the first black students admitted to prestigious Southwestern College (now Rhodes College) in Memphis. Cabbage went on to Morehouse College, where he was student government president.

Both Cabbage and Coby Smith had their baptism in Black Power while they were living in Atlanta. Cabbage was finishing his studies at Morehouse. Smith was dabbling in civil rights work, hanging out with Stokely Carmichael and other activists who identified with the Student Nonviolent Coordinating Committee.

SNCC had emerged in the early sixties as a youthful counterpoint to the SCLC. By the mid-sixties Carmichael was at the peak of his political influence as the chairman of SNCC. Under his leadership, the group embraced a black-nationalist agenda and demanded greater political and economic power for African Americans.

SNCC scorned King's bedrock principles of integration and nonviolence as too conservative to advance the movement further. It took on a more belligerent tone in May 1967 when H. Rap Brown replaced Stokely Carmichael as chairman. Brown escalated Black Power rhetoric by famously declaring that violence was "as American as cherry pie." He threatened that "if American cities don't come around . . . they should be burned down."[7]

Inspired by the call of Black Power, Cabbage and Coby Smith conceived a mini version of SNCC for Memphis that they named the Black Organizing Project. It would be a "liberation school" for youths, teaching black history and building racial pride.

Upon their return to Memphis, they roamed inner-city streets recruiting "brothers" to join their group. From the title of a popular TV show about hostile aliens descending upon Earth, they borrowed a new, more muscular name for themselves, the Invaders. Their network of activists was a loose-knit collection of people linked to what an FBI report termed Black Power "cells" of students at LeMoyne and Owen Colleges, Memphis State University, and local high schools, plus graduates and dropouts. All told, they totaled about seventy-five people, according to an FBI estimate.[8]

When the garbage workers' strike began, the Invaders saw an opportunity. By identifying with the goal of economic justice, they aimed to widen their influence. By 1968, another member of the Invaders, John Burl Smith, had emerged as a leader of the group. John Burl Smith, back in Memphis after a stint in the air force, seemed to borrow from H. Rap Brown's rhetoric. He developed what he called an "armed wing" of the Invaders and implied that they ought to equip themselves with guns.[9]

The Invaders turned up at meetings of the Community on the Move for Equality, known as COME, the strike-support group led by Reverend Jim Lawson. In the early days of the strike, Cabbage and several other Invaders were involved in COME's deliberations. At a meeting of COME on March 5, Cabbage defied the organization's principle of nonviolent protest by circulating a flyer by H. Rap Brown that included instructions for making a Molotov cocktail.[10] John Burl Smith rattled another COME meeting by scorning it as nothing more than a group of "ministers praying." If the ministers meant business, Smith went on, they had to "do some fighting."[11] Lawson soon lost patience with the Invaders and paid them little mind at meetings.[12] Feeling slighted and resentful, Cabbage stopped attending.

Lawson privately expressed his disgust with the Invaders as a "divergent, dissident, belligerent group" that did nothing except "beg money without offering anything constructive."[13] Lawson's low opinion of the Invaders did not bode well for King's effort to recruit them. Lawson nonetheless suspended his disbelief that the Invaders would fall in line behind King. If King was determined to recruit the Invaders as part of a united community front behind the upcoming march, Lawson said he would go along with it.

King supposed that he could win the allegiance of Black Power militants by the force of his arguments for nonviolence. First, he portrayed his brand of massive civil disobedience as radical in its own way. It was not passive. It relied on massive "militant" (his word) confrontation and protest. Second, he dismissed as fantasy the idea of armed revolution that some Black Power extremists were envisioning in their rhetoric. He would test the strategy in Memphis.

If the strategy worked in Memphis, King might conclude that it would work with Black Power militants who might otherwise disrupt the Poor People's Campaign in Washington. Heading off a threat to the Poor People's Campaign was not the only reason that King sought to bring Black Power militants under his wing. Black Power was commanding the media spotlight. Its energy, fueled by anger and revolutionary zeal, was captivating and radicalizing black youth.

His strategy rested on the premise that he could repeat elsewhere what he had achieved in Chicago. How complete a conversion of the gangs he had achieved in Chicago, however, was never clear. Years later, Ralph Abernathy would look back on King's earnest efforts as having been largely a bust. Abernathy's recollection was very different from King's: "Martin had encountered for the first time a crowd of blacks that he could neither reason with nor overpower with his philosophy."[14]

In Abernathy's telling, King's approach to the gangs was doomed from the start because the gang members were devoid of "respect for anything or anybody, most especially for preachers." Historian Fairclough agrees, saying that many of the gang members with whom King rapped for hours remained "cynically aloof."[15]

Now in Memphis, applying the lesson of Chicago, he courted the Invaders. But the Invaders differed from the Blackstone Rangers. The Invaders were not poorly educated, ghettoized toughs engaged in drug trafficking or other criminal enterprise. Cabbage's group had no criminal intent. The Invaders were led by college students or graduates steeped in SNCC rhetoric. Their motivation was Black Power ideology.

In recruiting the Invaders, King would not be filling an ideological void, as he had with the Chicago gangs. He would have to confront the Invaders' radicalism head-on and rebut their conviction that King's nonviolence was feckless, that its time was past. To dissuade them was to dispute the idea at the crux of Black Power. In Chicago, King and his aides had spent much of one summer working to gain the gangs' allegiance. In Memphis they had less than a week.

At 3:17 p.m., Monday, April 3, King left the meeting with Lucius Burch. He headed to the motel's dining room, where he found Cabbage, John Burl Smith, and about fifteen other Invaders seated in chairs.[16] King sat down facing them. Even sitting, the lanky Cabbage loomed over King. Cabbage was wearing blue jeans, a sweatshirt, and sandals. The same clothes had served as his virtual uniform for the preceding year. He owned just one pair of blue jeans, and he and other Invaders were struggling to feed themselves for lack of money.[17]

King asked Cabbage's group if they could agree to a pledge of nonviolence.[18] The Invaders evaded the question but portrayed themselves as the key to a peaceful march in Memphis. They argued that King ought to work with them because they had grassroots support in the African American community. They faulted Jim Lawson for not including them in COME's planning before the march of March 28. As one Invader recounted years later, they said that, if King had met with the Invaders early on, the march would have been "free of violence."[19] On the strength of that claim, the Invaders repeated their demand for money to fund their Black Organizing Project. King seemed sympathetic. Emboldened, Cabbage asked for $2 million, according to an account of an FBI informant.[20] The sum far exceeded the SCLC's total annual budget.

King did not promise to tap SCLC's treasury to fund any of the Invaders' programs. He said, however, that he would try to find other sources of money. He mentioned a coalition of black churches that had established a fund-raising arm to aid militant black groups. To show that he meant business, King picked up the telephone right then and called a number in New York. "Okay," he told Cabbage a moment later, "we have a commitment to partially fund your program."[21]

For his part King asked the Invaders to make the rounds of the city's black high schools and urge the students' cooperation to keep Monday's march peaceful.[22] He asked that the Invaders provide at least twenty-five of their members to serve as parade marshals.[23] When King again demanded a pledge of nonviolence, Cabbage hedged. "We told him, okay, we will try to do our best," Cabbage would recall. "We will try to do this, even though we can't guarantee that violence will not break out."[24] On that note the meeting with the Invaders ended at about 4:30 p.m.

Chapter 11

Nine-to-Five Security

*I can't lead that kind of life. I'd feel like a bird
in a cage. . . . There's no way in the world you can keep
somebody from killing you if they really want to kill you.*

—MLK, responding to a plea that he travel
with bodyguards, Albany, Georgia, March 23, 1968

EXHAUSTED AT THE END OF A DAY of travel and high-stakes meetings, King returned to his room to rest. Despite his outward calmness at the time, the bomb threat to his flight that morning was still eating at him. That would become painfully evident in an emotional speech that he would deliver that night.

The bomb scare appeared to have struck him as a dire warning about the perils awaiting him in Memphis. If he could not say who or when someone might attack, he knew that he was in mortal danger. Would his assailant be an extremist pro-war hawk aggrieved by his denunciation of US policy in Vietnam? Might it be a law-and-order zealot outraged by his vow to hound and disrupt Washington for the poor? Perhaps a trigger-happy racist inflamed by loathing for him and everything he personified? Or a Black Power fanatic targeting a man he perceived as an anti-revolutionary?

Being in Memphis was doing nothing to allay King's fear. The city was very much on edge, the racial tensions from the strike sharpened by continuing bitterness over the riot and the harsh police response to it. Anxiety was in the air, and King was being swept into it. John Lewis, the young movement leader who was working in tandem with the SCLC, was hearing reports from people close to King that he was seized by dread. Lewis would later recall learning that King was anguished by "the ugliness and killing that was rising up all around him. He could feel it closing in."[1]

King's fear for his safety in Memphis was in no way alarmist. It was well founded, as the police were aware. Even before King's visits to the city on March 18 and March 28, the Memphis police were fielding threats against him.[2] According to Memphis police director Frank Holloman, police headquarters and other city agencies had been receiving calls warning that "something was liable to happen to Dr. King."[3]

Holloman nevertheless decided against providing security for King on either March 18 or 28. In congressional testimony in 1978, Holloman explained why. He said of King: "He was just another person who was involved in the sanitation strike, and there was no reason, apparently, that we even thought of providing security for him."[4]

Nor did the Memphis authorities notify King of the threats against him. Or so it appears. In his testimony before the House Select Committee on Assassinations about the police handling of King's security, Holloman did not mention any such warnings having been conveyed to King in mid-March. More threats had poured in after the March 28 riot. The police evidently did not warn King of those threats either. An after-action report prepared by the police department detailing hour-by-hour the surveillance and security surrounding King's presence in Memphis on April 3 and 4 says nothing about warnings to him.[5]

It would seem that the bomb scare in Atlanta might have prompted him to request police protection in Memphis whether or not he knew of the threats. But he did not request a police bodyguard in Memphis. He rarely sought police protection, yet he feared that he could die a violent death at any moment.

He tried to buffer his fear by developing a numb fatalism, a defense against the dread that someone might kill him at any moment. If dying violently was inevitable, he reckoned, he might as well resign himself to it. He girded himself mentally against the nerve-racking despair of constant panic. "He was philosophical about his death," Andrew Young would recall. "He knew it would come, and he just decided, you know, there was nothing to do about it."[6]

When President Kennedy was slain in 1963, King told his wife, Coretta, that he expected the same fate for himself.[7] If the president had not been safe from an assassin's bullet, King confided to his aides, neither was he. From the time John Kennedy was killed, Andrew Young would remember, "Dr. King just felt, when your time comes, if the president can't be secured with hundreds of Secret Service, there's nothing that two or three officers are going do with us."[8]

As he traveled around the country, King declined many offers of police security. He did not want a phalanx of police hanging around him. He believed that having armed officers in uniform standing vigil over him would send the wrong message. His was a message of nonviolent protest, a Christian tenet of turning the other cheek to hatred and violence. It was a credo that clashed with the open display of armed police guards ready to shoot.

To look to the Memphis police in particular for protection must have struck King as a doubtful proposition. Undercover officers on Holloman's force were infiltrating the meetings of striking garbage workers and their supporters. The police were suspect in the eyes of the strike supporters for having employed harsh tactics to quell the rioting on March 28. Though many marchers had been teargassed and beaten, King had not. All the same, considering the conduct of the Memphis police that day, he had reason not to trust them.

In the days before King returned to the city on April 3, the number of death threats spiked higher.[9] According to Holloman, the authorities received a flurry of telephone calls to the effect that King "would not live through" the march of April 6. Holloman said in court testimony on April 4 that he was "very much concerned" about King's safety.[10]

The surge of threats and the rioting on March 28 had caused Holloman to reconsider his position that King did not warrant any special protection. Under the circumstances the police director had determined that prudence dictated a security detail for him. So it was that, when King arrived at the Memphis airport on April 3, Inspector Donald Smith's detail of four officers had been there to guard him.

Smith and the other officers remained on the King watch all day. At 5:05 p.m., Smith called headquarters for permission to "secure the detail"—police-speak for "end the mission." Permission was granted. That concluded the security for King, not just for that day but indefinitely. There was no security detail assigned to protect him that night or the next day.[11] The security shield for King, such as it was, had been in effect six hours and thirty-two minutes.

Why the security detail was disbanded at 5:05 p.m. on that Wednesday is a mystery. The after-action report, the police department's most complete review of its security for King during the visit in April 1968, does not say why. The report notes only that Chief J. C. MacDonald, who worked under Holloman's command, ordered the security detail to stand down at 5:05 p.m.[12] Holloman would say later that he did not remember having authorized the stand-down. In his testimony he conceded that abandoning security on the afternoon of King's first day in Memphis was "not proper considering the circumstances."[13]

Holloman's testimony revealed the low priority that he had assigned to King's security. He said that he had not involved himself in the particulars of the security plan for King on April 3. Nor had he monitored how things were going. Holloman's priority was surveillance, not security. The surveillance by officers Ed Redditt and Willie Richmond did not end on Wednesday afternoon. They returned to their post at the firehouse across Mulberry Street from the Lorraine the next morning.

Holloman acquired his training in law enforcement during his decades with the FBI under the surveillance-prone management of J. Edgar Hoover. Holloman joined the bureau in 1937 after graduating from the University of Mississippi Law School. He rose through the ranks, heading regional bureaus in Atlanta, Memphis, Cincinnati, and Jackson, Mississippi. In 1956, Hoover named him "inspector in charge" at FBI headquarters. In that position he oversaw FBI personnel for eight years, reporting to Hoover.

After Mayor Loeb appointed him to head the Memphis Police Department, in January 1968, Holloman moved swiftly to create an Inspectional Division. In effect it meant a new emphasis on covert operations. As he would explain later, Holloman had a "special interest" in developing the department's intelligence capacity.[14]

Holloman was taking a page from Hoover's playbook. The Inspectional Division was the Memphis version of the FBI's Intelligence Division. At Hoover's direction the FBI had launched, in the late 1950s, a secret program known as COINTELPRO (Counterintelligence Program). COINTELPRO officially existed to investigate communist activity, but it morphed into a mammoth "dirty tricks" operation to thwart supposedly radical elements in the civil rights movement. King was a major target.

When the garbage workers went on strike, Holloman assigned Redditt and Richmond to surveillance. He assigned Marrell McCollough, a recent police recruit, to undercover work, tasking him to infiltrate the Invaders. Like Redditt and Richmond, McCollough was an African American. No African Americans were assigned to Detective Smith's security detail.

Holloman's emphasis on surveillance over security in King's case seemed in line with his enthusiasm for counterintelligence. In defending his policy years later, Holloman would say that, had King agreed to cooperate, the police would have provided security for him the whole time he was in Memphis. Without that cooperation, Holloman said, he did not think that a security detail would have served any purpose.[15]

In some other cities, however, law enforcement officials did not take no for an answer. They persuaded King to cooperate or provided security regardless. FBI records show that security measures for King were put into effect in a number of cities—from Milwaukee to Cincinnati, Boston to Las Vegas.

Even in die-hard segregationist Albany, Georgia, Chief Laurie Pritchett commenced round-the-clock police protection for King. Though King objected, Pritchett ignored him. The chief recognized the great risk to his city and his reputation if the nation's leading civil rights champion should die a violent death in Albany. According to an account by historian Stephen Oates, Pritchett declared that if King were murdered in Albany, "the fires would never cease."[16]

In 1964, during King's visit to Las Vegas, sheriff's deputies kept him under constant guard by day, and they stood vigil in his hotel suite at night.[17] In Los Angeles on February 28, 1965, one hundred police officers were deployed to protect him.[18] In Charlotte, North Carolina, where he attended a two-day conference in September 1966, Police Chief John Ingersoll assigned fourteen African American policemen to a security detail for King. As he left a speaking engagement, the officers held hands and formed a human corridor to shield him.

As recently as February, a few weeks before King's return to Memphis in April, police officers stood guard in the hallway leading to his room at the Sheraton Four Ambassadors Hotel in Miami. Apparently alarmed by death threats, the police prevailed on King to cancel a speech scheduled at Miami Beach and remain in the hotel. King complied.[19] Billy Kyles, the Memphis minister who was at the conference, would recall: "The Miami police begged Martin not to leave the hotel because there were so many threats against him. So we stayed inside."[20]

That's the sort of caution that Holloman's predecessor as head of the Memphis police, Claude Armour, had exercised during King's 1966 visit to Memphis. In the early 1960s, an era of court-ordered desegregation of schools and other public facilities, he decreed that his officers would follow the law and prevent any outbreak of violence. In the words of Maxine Smith, the executive director of the Memphis branch of the NAACP at the time: "He let his force know that he would not tolerate anything. He was going to see to it that those kids got to school and got home safely, and he did that."[21]

Under Armour's stewardship of the department, however, allegations of police misconduct against African Americans did not cease. Maxine Smith accused the department of arresting blacks without cause in some instances and mistreating them. Smith said, "Police officers can do whatever they want to do under the guise of being police officers." The term "John Gaston turbans" came into currency among the city's defense lawyers. It was a reference to the many swaddled heads of blacks beaten by police and treated at the city's public John Gaston Hospital.[22] Young blacks had another term for the police violence: *blue crush*.

An incident during the summer of 1967 buttressed the claim that police, under Armour's stewardship, were brutalizing blacks in Memphis with impunity. One sweltering night the police arrested the wrong man for the robbery of a convenience store. That night Gregory Jaynes, a reporter for the *Commercial Appeal*, was working the pressroom at police headquarters. Through the wall he heard the police walloping the suspect in a room next to his. He grabbed a telephone and called Barney DuBois, the paper's rewrite man. "I put the receiver to the wall so Barney could hear the beating and back me up," Jaynes would relate years later. His story ran on the front page of the Sunday paper. Four police officers were suspended. There was a civil service hearing, but the officers were not prosecuted. "They let the cops go," Jaynes would recall.[23]

Despite the department's mixed record on racial matters under Armour, his handling of security for King reflected a caution that would be lacking in the department under Holloman. In June 1966 King operated out of Memphis while he took part in a march across Mississippi begun by James Meredith, the first black student admitted, in 1962, to the state's flagship university at Oxford. In his home state Meredith was staging what he called a "march against fear" to combat racism.

Armour was determined that no harm would come to King while he was in Memphis. He ordered a security detail of eight African American officers and issued strict instructions: they would keep King safe, or there would be hell to pay.[24] Jerry Dave Williams, a black homicide detective, was put in charge. "We would go in and check the rooms, make sure the telephone wasn't bugged, check under the beds, check everywhere. Then I would assign two officers outside his door. We would take turns every two hours through the night," Williams would say later.[25]

Detective Redditt was one of the eight officers in Williams's detail. Armour took it upon himself to issue orders to Redditt. He summoned Redditt to his office. Redditt would remember Armour saying, "This man is an international figure, and you better not let anything happen to him. If something happens, you lose your badge."[26]

Guarding King had been unlike any other duty that Detective Redditt had performed as a police officer. King was staying at the Lorraine, where he had his customary Room 306 on the second floor. Wiry and fleet-footed (he had been a star sprinter on the track team at Manassas High School), Redditt had positioned his body as a human shield for King.

When King would leave his room to descend the open stairway to the ground floor, Redditt and other officers in the security detail were standing by. In Redditt's telling: "We had to put our bodies around him and walk him down the stairs." One morning, while King was eating breakfast, Redditt joked about all the trips up and down the stairs. "Why don't you get another room?" he asked King. "It's killing me walking up and down those steps."[27]

But Holloman did not follow Armour's example. He did not see security for King as a critical matter demanding his close attention and scrutiny. In sharp contrast to Armour's diligence in safeguarding King from harm, Holloman's attitude was passive, halfhearted. As a consequence, King was in greater jeopardy on April 4, 1968.

Chapter 12

Reluctant Speaker

*The time has come for us to civilize ourselves by the
total, direct and immediate abolition of poverty.*

—MLK, in his book *Where Do We Go from Here*,
published in June 1967

THAT NIGHT IT SEEMED that even the Lord was turning against King.
From inside his room at the Lorraine, he could hear the insistent wailing
of tornado sirens. The fury of the approaching storm gave him pause. He
doubted that much of a crowd would turn out for a speech on such a night.
He could picture yawning rows of empty seats in the vastness of Mason
Temple. If the crowd was paltry, if the rally was a bust, it would add to
his misery. Abernathy would recall King's hesitation: "It was clear that
few people would show up at the speech. Martin never liked to address
small crowds."[1]

King's health was another issue. He had a sore throat. His weeks of
breakneck travel pitching the Poor People's Campaign had worn him
down. He badly needed rest.

He knew from long experience that he would pay a price for subjecting
his body to punishing days on the road. He had a history of collapsing
from exhaustion. When he returned from the Nobel Peace Prize ceremony
in Oslo in 1964, he was brimming with pride but so fatigued that he had
checked into an Atlanta hospital.[2] Two years later, succumbing to what
Abernathy called "his virus," meaning the utter exhaustion and fever that
struck him in times of great stress, he missed most of the SCLC's annual

convention in Jackson, Mississippi.[3] It was then, in February 1968, that on doctor's orders he sought refuge in Acapulco for a break from the relentless pace of the Poor People's Campaign.[4]

On occasion, according to Andrew Young, King feigned sickness so he could duck out of an unwelcome event.[5] This time, though, he was not faking. He had a sore throat, likely aggravated by his smoking habit (a pack a day of Salems), and he was not feeling well.[6]

Sleepless nights worsened his exhaustion. Toward the end of March, as he wrapped up a busy round of recruiting in Harlem and Newark for the Poor People's Campaign before the rush back to Memphis, he was laboring under a severe sleep deficit. He told a reporter, "I've been getting two hours of sleep a night for the past ten days."[7]

King suffered from migraine headaches and chronic insomnia.[8] He tried sleeping pills, but they no longer worked for him. It was "Martin's war on sleep," Abernathy would say.[9] Some of his aides were night owls too and would sit with him, talking into the wee hours through whatever issues were bedeviling him. As Andrew Young put it, "We almost always ran relays keeping him company."[10] His aides suspected that his bouts of depression, which hit him in moments of extreme sadness and even great joy, might have been at the root of the insomnia.[11]

Even if he could overcome the exhaustion and acquit himself well in Mason Temple that night, King worried how the media would play his speech. If the crowd were to be small, reporters might ask embarrassing questions: Why had so many more people turned up for his speech on March 18? Was the storm howling outside the sole explanation? Had the rioting in Memphis on March 28 degraded King's support in the pro-strike community?

He was acutely aware of how he and his campaigns would play in newspapers and on TV screens. In his rise to national prominence King owed much of his success to media coverage. The emotional intensity of television operated as a crucial prop. King was savvy enough to recognize the potential of TV as an ally, and he and his aides tailored their strategy to exploit its power to the fullest. Journalist David Halberstam even portrayed the civil rights movement under King as "a great televised morality play."[12]

In Birmingham the seduction of TV cameras had contributed to King's decision to mobilize high school students as demonstrators. To have police dogs snapping at young marchers was bound to produce dramatic footage. It was a shrewd, though controversial, tactic. It would expose children to the risk of a violent police response. Andrew Young would explain years later how much the lure of television coverage shaped SCLC strategy: "During the Birmingham campaign we would schedule demonstrations in the morning in order to leave time for the national TV networks to ship film footage out on the 2 p.m. flight to New York. The footage would arrive in time for the networks to produce it for their evening news shows."[13]

But by 1968 the media spotlight was on urban rioting and Black Power militancy. The thrust of the coverage was negative. Media interest in King's comparatively moderate message of nonviolent protest was waning. Mostly his antiwar utterances gained much traction, and it was largely critical. Other than the riot on March 28, the Memphis story was capturing little national media coverage. As Jesse Jackson would recount: "Memphis was an isolated area, the media wasn't there, and we were already in a media slump. They had about locked Martin out of the press, and the Memphis garbage workers could only be a small space at best."[14]

King had no reason to expect that many reporters would turn up at Mason Temple on the stormy night of April 3. The opposite was more likely. There might not be any TV cameras or national reporters on hand, and there would probably be only a few local ones. Maybe none. It was a disheartening thought.

Given the dim prospects, he was uneasy about speaking at all that night. He decided not to go. Instead he would stay in his room and rest.

He told Abernathy, "I really don't feel like speaking."

Abernathy replied, "Why don't you let Jesse go? He loves to speak."[15]

No, King said. He was wary of Jackson's outsize ambition and did not want the charismatic twenty-six-year-old spellbinder filling in for him. He asked Abernathy to speak. "Can I take Jackson along?" Abernathy asked.

"Yes, but you do the speaking," King insisted.[16]

So, with Jackson and Young in tow, Abernathy drove through slashing rain to Mason Temple.

Alone in Room 306, King telephoned SCLC board member Marian Logan in New York City. King and Logan had been arguing about the Poor People's Campaign for weeks. Logan and her husband, Arthur, were close friends of King and longtime financial supporters of the SCLC. King so valued their friendship that he had invited them, as part of a select group of family and close associates, to be on hand in Oslo when he was awarded the Nobel Peace Prize.

The Logans were unlike many of King's close friends. They lived out-side the South. Neither was a minister. Arthur Logan was a well-regarded surgeon and civic leader in New York. One of his patients was jazz great Duke Ellington. Marian herself had been a fine cabaret singer. It was a measure of King's esteem for her that he had asked her to join the SCLC board. On the board she was unique in two respects: the only woman and the only Northerner. She was avidly devoted to King and his nonviolent movement.

But when King embraced causes beyond his core civil rights mission, he no longer enjoyed Marian Logan's unwavering support. The Poor People's Campaign struck Logan as a great mistake. Ordinarily, if she had a bone to pick with King, she would do it privately. But she felt so strongly about the Poor People's Campaign that on March 8 she had fired off a six-page memo to King and the other SCLC board members detailing her objections.

Bluntly she told them it was not the time for thousands of poor people to besiege the nation's capital. Many Americans were already angry about rioting in urban ghettos. She noted the "climate of confusion, splinter-ing, backlash and reaction that reigns over the country at present."[17] She expected that King's confrontational tactics would not sway Congress to authorize programs for the poor but rather would harden its opposition to them. As she told him, she believed his antipoverty campaign was crudely planned and would fail "to move the conscience of the Congress."[18] She predicted instead that the militant and disruptive (if nonviolent) demon-strations vowed by King would play into the hands of conservative, law-and-order candidates by fueling voters' support for them at the polls.

On the evening of Monday, March 25, having wound up a speaking tour in the East, King showed up unannounced at the Logans' brownstone on West Eighty-Eighth Street. He and Marian were soon hard at it, resuming their debate about the Poor People's Campaign. As journalist and author Gerold Frank would portray King that night, he lounged on a couch, his shoes and tie off. Fortified by copious amounts of orange juice and vodka, he jousted nonstop with Logan until almost dawn. Despite naysayers' ar-guments against his Washington plan, he told Logan, he would trust his instincts. If he had not trusted his instincts, he said, there would have been no Montgomery, no Selma, no Birmingham.[19]

Logan would relate, years later, the way the marathon session had ended: "Finally my husband said, 'Martin, leave her alone. You know, she's not gonna change her mind. She believes in this very strongly, and I think you should accept it.'"[20]

King quit the Logans' apartment that morning, but he wouldn't let the matter drop. Over the next week he called Logan almost every night. In the motel room on the evening of April 3 he called again, wheedling and badgering her, imploring her to side with him, begging her to trust his judgment.

Logan had the utmost respect for King. She revered him for his genial manner, sense of humor, profound moral sensibility, and oratorical genius. She would tell a reporter: "He was a brilliant man. I don't need to tell you how he could speak."[21]

But his outspoken opposition to the Vietnam War was troubling to her. Like several other close friends of King's, she feared that his antiwar stand would anger President Johnson and result in the loss of White House support for civil rights.

Moreover, she questioned King's judgment in reorienting the SCLC to fight against poverty. On that Monday night in New York, King had pressed her to see the logic, *his* logic, for the Poor People's Campaign. The harder he argued, the more she objected. She restated her concern: he should stick to racial progress for African Americans as his central cause, not pursue broad political and economic relief for all poor Americans. King's plan for Washington protest seemed to her unwieldy and unrealistic. She believed, as she put it, "We had bitten off a lot more than we were going to be able to chew."[22]

Logan had only to read the charter of the SCLC, which was founded in 1957, to see how the organization's scope under King's leadership had widened. The charter stated: "SCLC has the basic aim of achieving full citizenship rights, equality, and the integration of the Negro in all aspects of American life."[23] King had led the SCLC in that spirit for a decade in the push to desegregate public facilities and secure voting rights for African Americans. The charter said nothing about ending poverty for all Americans.

Having achieved much of his civil rights agenda in the South, King had reset the SCLC's agenda. He shifted its focus to remedy what he viewed as the nation's next great social injustice: the poverty afflicting millions of people, including a disproportionate number of African Americans. He often summed up his thinking with a snappy one-liner: "What does it profit a man to be able to sit at an integrated lunch counter if he doesn't earn enough money to buy a hamburger and a cup of coffee."[24]

King's pivot to economic justice did not happen overnight. At least as early as his graduate study at Crozer Theological Seminary in Upland, Pennsylvania, the nineteen-year-old King identified helping poor people as a goal he aspired to pursue. In a paper during his first semester he vowed that he would be a "profound advocate" on behalf of the poor.[25] Two developments in the mid-sixties had propelled him to convert the desire into action. First there was the explosion of civil strife in the Watts section of Los Angeles in 1965, followed by rioting in scores of other cities during the next two summers. Second was the futility of his quest, in 1966, to better the condition of Chicago's slums.

Chicago taught him that racism was subtler and less visible in cities beyond the South. The object was not desegregating restaurants and movie theaters but improving housing, education, and employment opportunity for African Americans. In Chicago inner-city blacks were caught in a complex web of poverty. Without a radical fix, he concluded, there was no escape.

In early 1968 he announced a fully developed plan of action. He had previewed his thinking in his book published six months before, *Where Do We Go from Here: Chaos or Community?* In the book he urged nothing less than the "radical restructuring of the architecture of American society."[26] The restructuring he proposed would end poverty simply by ending it legislatively—that is, by guaranteeing a minimum income for all Americans. For those who could work, it would provide a job. For those who could not, it would provide an income pegged to the median income nationwide.[27] In his thinking, the guarantee of a minimum income or a job did not go far enough. He called, further, for massive federal spending on housing and education.

It all was part of what he termed an Economic Bill of Rights for the Disadvantaged. It would not be cheap. King envisioned a federal antipoverty budget of ten or twelve billion dollars.[28] By contrast, President Johnson's "war on poverty," which he had launched in 1965, cost $2.4 billion a year (pared to $1.8 billion in later years owing to the fiscal drain of the Vietnam War).

The Poor People's Campaign was to be King's lever to force the government to abolish poverty. The campaign was modeled on the Depression-era march of fifteen thousand World War I veterans to Washington in 1932. The veterans, known as the Bonus Army, had flooded into the nation's capital demanding the bonuses promised to them by the federal government but never paid. They had slapped together shantytowns—Hoovervilles, critics mockingly called them. The veterans declared their intention to remain until Congress and President Herbert Hoover approved the bonuses, but Congress had not complied. His patience at an end, Hoover summoned the army to remove two thousand veterans still refusing to budge from the shantytowns. Soldiers routed the holdouts with tear gas and drove them out of Washington.

Marian Logan suspected that the Poor People's Campaign would end just as badly.[29] King would be mustering thousands of impoverished people from around the country for weeks of protest. They would represent a racial, cultural, and geographic hodgepodge. King was threatening to close down the seat of the federal government.[30] He was pledging nonviolence, but like NAACP leader Roy Wilkins, Logan doubted King could prevent violent incidents from erupting during the Washington protest. King was charting a prolonged siege of the capital, promising massive, disruptive civil disobedience. "I can't imagine a situation more flammable," Logan wrote in her memo.[31]

Even as he was preparing to besiege Washington, King's political ideology was shifting leftward. He kept his most radical views out of the public eye, but he confided to aides and friends that he had little faith in capitalism to lift people out of poverty. In a private meeting with SCLC staff, in December 1967, he spoke about capitalism and socialism. According to historian David Garrow, King said that he "didn't believe that capitalism, as it was constructed, could meet the needs of poor people, and that what we might need to look at was a kind of socialism, but a democratic form of socialism."[32]

So strongly did he hold that view that he berated Andrew Young for lacking it. King and his close aide were attending a party at Harry Belafonte's apartment in New York. It was March 27, two days after King's all-night session with Marian Logan. King was in a sour mood, expressing his sympathy with the rage of inner-city youths and fuming that the "system" was to blame.

Young commented, as quoted by Belafonte in the singer's memoir: "Well, I don't know, Martin. It's not the entire system. It's only part of it, and I think we can fix that."

King snapped at him: "I don't need to hear from you, Andy. I've heard enough from you. You're a capitalist, and I'm not."[33]

King objected to the capitalist economic model because he doubted that it alone would spread wealth fairly and widely. His view was not absolute. He valued a zone of private enterprise as a ladder of opportunity for African Americans. Franchising fast-food outlets he saw as one such ladder, as did his friend Judge Ben Hooks of Memphis. In 1968, Hooks and famed gospel singer Mahalia Jackson were building a chain of black-owned chicken restaurants. They had franchised more than twenty of the fast-food outlets under the name of Mahalia Jackson's Glori-Fried Chicken. According to Hooks, King was intrigued by the Mahalia Jackson concept because he saw it as a potential form of "economic power" enabling African Americans to own franchised businesses.

By the spring of 1968 King was speaking and writing sharply, harshly, to deplore economic injustice. His manner marked a departure from what he had exhibited as a young civil rights leader. The tone of the younger King had been gentle and reassuring. He had talked of goodness as the guiding light of the movement. He had talked of Christian love, the spirit of reconciliation, and the promise of beloved communities. He had endorsed moderation. As he told students at the University of California at Berkeley, in 1957: "If moderation means moving on with wise restraint and calm reasonableness, then moderation is a great virtue."[34]

Reassuring words about a commitment to wise restraint would have been welcome to Logan in 1968. King's dispute with Logan and his caustic words for Young showed how far his center of political gravity had shifted. He and Logan seemed to turn a deaf ear to the other's arguments. Her haggling with him over the Poor People's Campaign was a continual burden on him. It was yet another weight on his spirits when he was already feeling crushing pressure from all sides in Memphis.

Chapter 13

The Stalker

To this day the white poor also suffer deprivation
and the humiliation of poverty, if not of color.

—MLK, in his book *Why We Can't Wait*,
published in 1963

DESPITE THE NAME, the New Rebel Motor Hotel was not so much a hotel as a forty-two-room motel on the southern outskirts of Memphis. It stood just inside the city limits facing the road known both as Highway 78 and Lamar Avenue. Highway 78 was a main artery from the Deep South. For travelers from Birmingham (250 miles to the southeast) and Atlanta (155 miles beyond), it offered a straight shot to Memphis.

Looming over the motel was a gleaming, red-and-white sign proclaiming its name. The sign beckoned to travelers arriving from the Deep South, for whom the name must have struck a sympathetic chord. The name New Rebel evoked not just old-fashioned nostalgia but also the defiant battle cry of the old Confederacy. Lest there be any doubt about its down-in-Dixie essence, the motel created its own postcards to underscore the theme. The postcards boasted: "Home of Southern Hospitality."

It was 7:15 in the evening of April 3, as the sky was turning black and the air blustery, when a Ford Mustang pulled off Highway 78 and halted at the New Rebel. In the dim light the Mustang, a pale yellow, looked white or off-white. On the rear of the car was a red-and-white Alabama license plate. A Mexican visa sticker labeled "Turista" adorned the windshield.

A slender, dark-haired man of medium height exited the Mustang into the chill air and entered the office of the New Rebel. He was of medium height. He had a long, sharp nose and a cleft chin. He had turned forty less than a month before, but he looked at least a few years younger. He was wearing a somber business suit, white shirt, and dark, narrow knit tie.

The man asked the motel's desk clerk, Henrietta Hagemaster, for a room. The rate was $6.24 a night. On a registration card the man scrawled the name Eric S. Galt and the address 2608 Highland Avenue, Birmingham. He was checked in to Room 34.

The roughhewn twang of the few words the man spoke to Hagemaster seemed to peg him as a Southerner of humble origins. In the months to come, the FBI would interview lots of people who had encountered the man in the months before he arrived in Memphis. Something had been puzzling about him. He did not seem to fit into an obvious occupational category. Probably an accountant, one person said. He looked "for all the world like a preacher," another said.[1]

He was not an accountant, a preacher, or a Southerner. His real name was not Eric S. Galt. It was James Earl Ray. Outwardly he appeared fairly well off, but it was not so. There was a hidden side to him, even in the matter of his clothes. As an FBI report would indicate, not all of his clothes were as fine as his suit and knit tie. He had extended the life of his undershorts by mending them by hand in two places with brown thread.

Ray was born on March 10, 1928, in Alton, Illinois. Located fifteen miles north of St. Louis along the Mississippi River, Alton was then a decaying industrial town on the brink of the Great Depression. He grew up in abject poverty in Alton and in nearby, blue-highway pockets of southeastern Illinois and eastern Missouri. His early years epitomized American poverty and family dysfunction at its worst.

Ray's wretched background and the hardships of his youth could have been a case in point for Martin Luther King Jr. If King had known of the toxic circumstances of Ray's youth, he might have cited them as an example of the kind of corrosive poverty that compelled him to embark on the Poor People's Campaign.

Ray was the oldest of nine children born to Lucille and George Ray. Derisively nicknamed "Speedy" because of his sluggish speech, George never was much of a breadwinner. He had bounced from one job to another.[2] He was an auto mechanic, used-car salesman, railroad brakeman, and carnival fighter, but nothing lasted long. With little or no money coming in, the family was so poor that sometimes they had only potatoes to eat.[3] Lucille, who was known as Ceal, coped as best she could or, when she couldn't anymore, turned to drink.

By the time Ray was in the first grade, the family had retreated to a dilapidated, tin-roof house on a meager farm near the rural hamlet of Ewing, Missouri, population 324. Farming on their infertile land did not pay any better than Speedy's modest jobs. Ceal hated country life.

At the Ewing Consolidated Elementary School, James Ray was often the target of ridicule among his classmates. He was painfully shy. Often his clothes were tattered, dirty, and foul-smelling. He did poorly in his studies, though he would test with an average 108 IQ.[4] Eight years of schooling was all he could stand, as he would say later.[5]

As Ray grew older, his life did not get better. It got worse. In his vivid biography, Gerald Posner explains that "there was no guidance in the Ray household, no family member to whom any of the children could look for inspiration, no encouragement to do well at school or to make friends, and no role model who showed it was possible to work honestly and diligently to pull oneself out of poverty." The Rays reached a point of such desperation that they burned their house piecemeal to stay alive. As Posner describes it: "In 1940 when James was twelve, the Rays began slowly cannibalizing their decrepit house, pulling it apart plank by plank in order to use it as firewood. It gradually disintegrated until they needed a new home."[6]

During that time, Ray had his first brush with the law. He was only eleven when he and his brother John grabbed a stack of newspapers deposited by a truck on a street corner for distribution. The Ray brothers were caught and briefly jailed, but the police let them off with only a warning.

In 1951, Ray's parents separated. By then Speedy had taken up with another woman and Ceal had sunk into utter despair. In her last years she was reduced to loitering in bars or being hauled off by police for drunkenness and disorderly conduct.[7] She died of acute alcoholism in 1953.

Most of her children fared no better. All the children were apart from their mother by the age of sixteen.[8] One of Ray's sisters, Marjorie, was six when she burned to death from a fire that she started while playing with matches. Max had severe mental disabilities and was placed in a special home in Aton. Suzan and Franklin were taken from Ceal by court order and placed in a Catholic home in Springfield, Missouri. Melba, who suffered from emotional distress, ended up in a mental institution.[9]

Ceal's trouble with the law stemming from poverty and alcoholism paled next to the criminality of her family. When Speedy was twenty-one, before marrying Ceal, he was convicted of breaking and entering, a felony. He served two years in the Iowa State Penitentiary at Fort Madison. A long string of crimes committed by Speedy's brother, Earl (the inspiration for James's middle name), including rape, put him behind bars for most of his adult life.[10]

Two of Ray's brothers, Jerry and John, seemed to follow in Speedy's and Uncle Earl's footsteps. Jerry was sent to a reformatory at fourteen for mugging drunks and snatching purses. Within a month of his release, he was back in prison for grand larceny. At nineteen, John robbed a gas station and was sentenced to two to five years in the Indiana State Penitentiary at Pendleton.[11]

If Ray seemed destined for a life of crime, he did try to follow a different path. When he was sixteen, he moved to Alton and found work in the dye room of the International Shoe Tannery. Laid off by the tannery, he enlisted in the army at age seventeen.

Military service, however, did not suit him. He showed his contempt for military discipline by flouting the army's rules of conduct. While stationed in Germany, he peddled cigarettes on the black market. Against army regulations he drank "in quarters"—that is, in the barracks. In a final act of defiance, he went AWOL. He was quickly apprehended and court-martialed. He did not fail at everything in the military. In basic training he qualified for the marksman's medal, a classification of proficiency, though below the levels of sharpshooter and expert.[12] On December 10, 1948, he was discharged from the army for "ineptness and lack of adaptability to military service."[13]

Back in the States, Ray found work at the Dryden Rubber Company in Chicago. It was another factory job, honest work, but he was let go after three months. With little money and at loose ends, he jumped freight trains, riding the rails all the way to Los Angeles.

Alone in a city that must have seemed like another world to him, he was soon in trouble. On the night of October 7, 1949, he attempted to rob the upstairs office of a cafeteria, the Forum. The manager spotted him crouched behind a safe. Ray fled, outrunning a parking attendant. Recklessly, he returned to the same area four days later. The parking attendant called the police. Ray denied everything, but he was convicted of second-degree burglary and served ninety days in the county jail.[14]

He retreated to Chicago, seemingly determined to stay on the right side of the law. He took an assembly-line job in one factory, then two more in succession. He enrolled in a course for a high school equivalency degree. He kept at it for two years before his tolerance for tedious, low-wage jobs reached a limit. He went AWOL, this time not from the army but from his job in the envelope-manufacturing department at Avery Corporation.

With no means of support, on May 6, 1952, he attempted to hold up a taxi driver with a pistol. He meant to hijack the taxi. The driver foiled him by grabbing the keys. Ray fled. A bystander raced after him and alerted police, who gave chase. In the melee that followed, Ray was shot in the arm and arrested.[15]

He was twenty-four, a high school dropout, a flop as a soldier, a jobless loner encumbered by a criminal record and unmoored from family. It seemed to mark a moment of final surrender. He slumped into the life of a drifter and habitual outlaw. As Percy Foreman, one of Ray's eventual lawyers, would put it: "He called his pistol his credit card and committed a robbery every time he came into a new city."[16]

For years Ray pulled off a string of petty robberies, many with impunity. At other times he bungled them. A bonehead attempt to burglarize a laundry in East Alton in 1954 ended in a comical snafu.[17] As Ray hoisted himself to a window at the laundry, his shoes stuck in deep mud. In 1959, he and an accomplice robbed an IGA food market in Alton, making off with nearly $1,000. At the wheel of the getaway car, Ray failed to shut the door on the driver's side. It swung open, and he almost fell out. With the police in hot pursuit he crashed the car into a tree.[18]

As his rap sheet lengthened, so did his prison terms. He served a year or more at two state prisons in Illinois and three years in the federal penitentiary at Leavenworth, Kansas. The stickup at gunpoint of a Kroger supermarket in St. Louis in July 1959 landed him in the Missouri State Penitentiary at Jefferson City facing a twenty-year sentence.

The arc of his life story seemed complete. He was a common criminal, a habitual offender in and out of prison. He had defined a criminal life for himself, but he was not good at it. In his many ill-conceived, botched attempts at crime, he showed he was "markedly inept," as Robert Blakey, chief counsel of the US House Select Committee on Assassinations, would observe years later.[19]

Doing hard time at Jeff City, as the maximum-security penitentiary was known, seemed to reshape his personality. He acquired a savvy and shrewdness that had not been evident before. That newfound capacity, combined with grit, enabled him to escape, Houdini-like, on April 23, 1967.

It was a Sunday. Ray was working his regular shift in the prison bakery, 11 a.m. to 7 p.m. A truck was to arrive that day to pick up bread for regular delivery to the honor farm beyond the prison gates. Ray contorted his five-ten frame under a false bottom of a metal breadbox that measured four feet long, three feet wide, and three feet deep. The box was meant for sixty loaves. A fellow inmate covered the false bottom with enough bread to camouflage his curled body below. When the truck arrived, two inmates rolled the breadbox into its cargo bay.

Once the truck cleared the gates, Ray unfolded himself from the box. He had planned carefully. He wore a dyed pair of black pants and white shirt under his orange prison uniform, which he quickly stripped off. When the truck stopped at an intersection, he leaped to the ground. He did not run but instead ambled off so as not to alert the driver.[20] He carried a stash of twenty candy bars, a comb, a razor and blades, a piece of mirror, soap, and a transistor radio.

According to his own eventual testimony, Ray laid low till dark, ducked through fields to avoid houses with lights, and trekked for seven nights, covering forty-five to sixty miles, and then jumped a railroad boxcar to St. Louis.[21] He had served seven years and thirty-seven days of his twenty-year sentence.

By July he managed to reach Canada, where the border with the United States was not then hard to cross for an American. In Montreal he tried and failed in his attempt to obtain a Canadian passport under the assumed name of Eric Starvo Galt, and he returned to Birmingham. There he answered an ad in the *Birmingham News* for a 1966 V-8 Mustang with whitewall tires. On August 30, posing as Galt, he bought the car for $1,966 cash.[22] Again using the Galt alias, he obtained an Alabama driver's license.

How Ray acquired the money to buy the Mustang and pay the thousands more that he spent while he was a fugitive would mystify investigators. One likely source was his hustling of drugs and other illicit goods at Jeff City, money he may have parked with his brothers while he was in prison. Another possibility was the armed $27,230 heist of the Bank of Alton, on July 13, 1967. It was an unsolved case in circumstances pointing vaguely to Ray. There were other lesser robberies for which he seemed a likely suspect, but no clear-cut evidence connected him to any of the thefts.

With the sporty Mustang as his calling card, Ray headed south and west. He clocked two thousand miles, eventually crossing the Rio Grande and going halfway down the Pacific coast of Mexico. He wound up in Puerto Vallarta, a derelict former mining town then emerging as an upscale beach resort.

Manuela Aguirre Medrano, a prostitute, would tell investigators that she and Ray became acquainted in Puerto Vallarta. She said that she slept with him several times while he was living high (beer during the day, gin at night). If anyone asked what he did for a living, he said he was a writer. He was calm, shy, yet prone to spew hatred against blacks, she would say of him.[23]

By mid-November, Ray was on the road again, back across the border and on to Los Angeles. He hung out in bars there, posturing as a businessman who had operated and sold a tavern in Mexico and who was mulling over his next venture. He embarked on a quirky quest for self-improvement. He hired a plastic surgeon to snub his pointy nose. He booked sessions with a psychologist and a hypnotist. He took courses in bartending and ballroom dancing. It was as though he was remaking himself for a more respectable calling. He devised a murderous plot instead.

Investigators who would inquire into Ray's life would find abundant evidence that he hated black people, King in particular.[24] Written on the back of his TV set they found the segregationist slur "Martin Luther Coon." They reported many instances in which Ray had allegedly uttered anti-black insults.[25] One of his lawyers, Percy Foreman, would say years later, "He is a racist, and has been one all his life. He could not think of anybody else not being a racist if they were white."[26]

While he was in Los Angeles, Ray's anti-black bigotry seemed to seize him with acute insistence. He circulated a petition to place third-party presidential candidate George Wallace, the segregationist former Alabama governor, on the California ballot. In one incident at a bar, the Rabbit Foot's Club, he had an angry exchange with a white woman, presumably over race. According to the bartender, Ray dragged the woman toward the door, hollering that he aimed to drop the woman off in Watts, the city's African American neighborhood.[27]

Just when Ray resolved to kill King remains an open question. In Los Angeles the idea stirred him into action. Perhaps not coincidentally, King was highly visible at the time, denouncing the Vietnam War and vowing massive demonstrations in Washington.

Over the weekend of March 16 to 17, King was in Los Angeles to preach at the Second Baptist Church. Ray, an avid newspaper reader, might well have seen articles in the Los Angeles press reporting King's visit and his plan to blitz the South later that week on behalf of the Poor People's Campaign.[28] Ray filled out a postal change-of-address form marked "General Delivery, Atlanta." On March 17, he left Los Angeles in the Mustang.

If Ray intended to head straight to Atlanta, he changed his mind. News media were reporting that King would travel to Selma, Alabama. Hot on King's trail, Ray drove to Selma. He spent the night of March 22, a Friday, at a motel in the Alabama city. But King was not in Selma that night. A last-minute change in his schedule had him sleeping in Camden, thirty-eight miles away.

Ray drove on to Atlanta. As was his habit on arriving in a new city, Ray looked for a cheap rooming house where he could stay. He found a room for $10.50 a week on Fourteenth Street near Piedmont Park, a Midtown area known as a hippie enclave.

He zeroed in on King's likely whereabouts. In pencil he circled a map of Atlanta at three points linked to King. One circle marked the SCLC headquarters, a second the Ebenezer Baptist Church, and the third a former house of King's. A fourth circle, around the Capitol Hill Housing Project, is where Ray would abandon his Mustang on April 5.

Ray outfitted himself in sniper mode. He shopped for a high-powered rifle, not in Atlanta but 150 miles away in Birmingham. For Ray, a felon using a fake name, Alabama was a less risky state than Georgia in which to buy a gun. In Alabama, unlike Georgia, there was no requirement that he identify himself.[29] He did not have to show his counterfeit driver's license, which would have identified him as Eric S. Galt. Keeping the transaction separate from his alias avoided creating a paper trail that might link the driver's license to the rifle that he intended to buy.

On Saturday, March 23, a week after his departure from Los Angeles, he drove to Birmingham to shop for the rifle. He parked the Mustang at the Aquamarine Supply Company, a sporting goods store opposite the Birmingham airport, and went inside.

He told the store manager, Donald Wood, that he wanted a rifle for deer hunting in Wisconsin. Ray selected a .30–06, pump-action Remington Gamemaster 760. The rifle could "drop a charging bull," according to Remington's marketing material.[30] Ray bought a Redfield 7x2 scope to attach to the Gamemaster. The scope would magnify an image to look seven times closer. He also bought a box of soft-point, military-style bullets, a kind that would mushroom on impact.[31] The total cost of the three purchases, plus tax, was $265.85. Ray signed the sales slip as Harvey Lowmeyer, thus distancing the alias of Eric S. Galt from the purchase of the rifle.

By Monday newspapers were reporting that King would return to Memphis that week to stage a nonviolent march. That same day, Ray left Atlanta for Tennessee. Where he stopped between Atlanta and Memphis is not known, although investigators would surmise that he paused somewhere, likely in a wooded area, for target practice.

On the outskirts of Memphis he found the New Rebel Motel and checked in. No one would report seeing Ray leave Room 34. At 10:20, during his evening rounds, night clerk Ivan Well would note that lights were burning brightly in Room 34. Ray may have been watching television. If so, he might have seen the late evening news on Channel Five, which reported King's arrival in Memphis that morning. A clip of the footage showed King entering Room 306 at the Lorraine.[32]

Chapter 14

Summoning Dr. King

*And so I call upon labor as the historic ally of the
underprivileged and oppressed to join with us in this
present struggle to redeem the soul of America.*

—MLK, speaking to the Illinois State AFL-CIO,
Springfield, Illinois, October 7, 1965

WHILE JAMES EARL RAY was holed up in the New Rebel Motel and a
thunderstorm was raging outside, hundreds of strikers and their supporters
were filtering into Mason Temple to hear King speak. They clustered in the
front section, shedding their rain-spattered jackets as they took their seats.
Looming above them was a raised platform from which King would speak.
All eyes were turned expectantly toward the front. King was not yet there.

Almost lost in the overwhelmingly African American crowd was a
sprinkling of white faces. Mike Cody, the young white lawyer assisting Lucius Burch to fight the federal injunction against King, was in the central,
main-floor section near the podium. That section of the auditorium was
packed with people. Cody would remember the air feeling stuffy, a sense
magnified by the fury of the storm outside, its thunder and lightning sti-
fling the crowd's murmuring to speakers' remarks from the podium.[1]

On this Wednesday night, though, the crowd filled at most half the seats
in the vastness of Mason Temple. Estimates of the turnout would range
from two thousand to four thousand.[2] In its edition the following morning
the *Commercial Appeal* would term the audience "disappointingly small."

The sparse turnout was a setback for the garbage workers, who had little reason to believe that their strike would end with a favorable outcome anytime soon. If they were losing heart, they were not without hope. They had faith that the man they knew reverently as Dr. King might somehow shift the momentum of the strike to save the day. (The honorific recognized the doctorate in systematic theology King earned at Boston University in 1955.)

Union leader Joe Warren would say: "We ain't never had a man, black or white [who was the equal of Dr. King]."[3] Taylor Rogers, another garbage worker in the crowd, would remember waiting eagerly to hear King speak again. Rogers had thrilled to King's speech on March 18. "It had ignited a much needed spark," he would later recall.[4]

The March 18 speech had boosted the strikers' spirits at a critical moment. Some workers who were initially on strike but who had returned to their jobs were so stirred by King's words that they had rejoined the strikers' ranks. Now Rogers was expecting another speech packed with power and emotion. He was praying that King's return to Memphis marked a turning point that would lead to victory for the strikers.

As the rally was getting under way, the storm bearing down on Memphis was lashing King's motel room with torrents of rain. He could hear the roar of thunder and see fearsome lightning strikes through the motel window. Worse, the scream of sirens continued to warn of tornadoes (which would strike nearby areas in Arkansas and West Tennessee, destroying houses and leaving two people dead and many injured).

Some Memphians were hunkered down at home. There were reasons other than the storm to stay put. For one, at 7:30 p.m., a revue of the talent acts in the upcoming Miss Memphis Pageant would be on television.

Mayor Loeb too was at home that night. Frank McRae telephoned him to tell his pal that he ought to expect a visit on Friday morning from a biracial delegation of Memphis pastors. The clergymen would be coming to city hall to question the mayor's unyielding attitude toward the strike. McRae asked if the mayor would receive the clergymen. "Fine," Loeb replied. "Be glad to see you, Frank. But you're going to waste your time, and all you're going to do is get yourselves in trouble with your congregations, and you're going to be misunderstood. You're not going to change my mind one way or another."[5]

Compared to many houses, Mason Temple offered a safe haven from tornadoes. But behind its brick facade it was nothing fancy. The seats were hard, straight-back, wooden chairs arrayed in semicircular rows under a lat-tice of steel girders. The official capacity was seventy-five hundred. Two or three thousand more, some standing, had somehow crammed into its two levels, a ground floor and balcony, for King's speech on March 18.

Entering the thick of a bitter labor strike like the one in Memphis was a rare, almost unprecedented step for King to take. Once, in 1964, he had briefly joined a picket line of workers on strike against a Scripto, Inc., facili-ity in his hometown of Atlanta.[6] For years he had courted unions in other ways. In a landmark pro-labor speech at the National AFL-CIO Con-vention at Bal Harbour, Florida, in 1961, King had proclaimed common cause between the labor and civil rights movements. On that occasion, he heralded the potential for unions to improve the wages and working con-ditions of African Americans. "If the Negro Wins, Labor Wins" was the title of the speech.[7]

A few unions with large black memberships had supported the SCLC financially. The United Packinghouse Workers of America had been a steady source of funds for the organization's often-depleted coffers. Walter Reuther of the United Automobile Workers was a fervent backer, and his union had been a major benefactor.[8]

But King's gratitude toward the labor movement had its limits. Many unions, particularly in the South, excluded blacks from membership and denied them apprenticeship training and vocational education.[9] King de-plored union racism, and he condemned it in no uncertain terms. In his 1958 book *Stride Toward Freedom*, King faulted those unions for having contributed to blacks' "degraded" economic circumstances.[10]

By 1968, however, as he looked for support in his fight against poverty, King seemed far more intent on promoting common cause with unions than decrying the racism that pervaded many of them. In *Where Do We Go from Here*, his blueprint for the Poor People's Campaign published in January 1968, King saluted unions for their increasing inclusion of African Americans.[11]

The turn of events in Memphis was drawing him into a closer embrace with the labor movement. If Memphis was risky for King, at least it offered a potential benefit. The more he advanced the unions' cause, the more likely they were to support his.

Now, at the rally in Mason Temple, King had the opportunity to lift the morale of one union, Local 1733 of AFSCME. With still no sight of King, other speakers bided time by warming up the crowd. They led them in prayer and song. They solicited strike-support donations. Jim Lawson took the podium and denounced the pending injunction against King, declaring, "Mace cannot stop us, gas cannot stop us, and we are going to march."[12]

Lawson reprised strike-related events of the previous few days. He denounced the police for employing what he regarded as brutally excessive force to quell the rioting on March 28. His voice ringing with indignation, Lawson accused one police officer of having fatally shot sixteen-year-old Larry Payne in cold blood.[13] Payne allegedly had looted a television from a Sears, Roebuck store before fleeing. A police department review would conclude later that in the aftermath of the riot Payne had pulled a knife on the patrolman, who shot in self-defense. The officer was exonerated. A number of witnesses, however, disputed the department's account.[14] According to historian Michael Honey, a dozen eyewitnesses said Payne had no knife but had his hands up and was killed by a blast from a shotgun poked into his stomach.[15]

Lawson was still addressing the crowd when Abernathy, Jackson, and Young entered through a side door of the temple. At the sight of them there was a great eruption of cheers and applause. They might have been rock stars leaping onto a stage. But as soon as it dawned on the crowd that King was not among them, the uproar fizzled as abruptly as it had begun. The crowd's message was unmistakable. "We said, 'It's not us they're cheering for.' We laughed about it, and we said he had to come," Jackson would recall.[16]

Years later, Abernathy would recap his thoughts at that moment. He would write in his memoir that the people "who had driven through rainy, windswept streets" to Mason Temple "had done so because they expected to see Martin Luther King, Jr., not Ralph D. Abernathy. I knew that better than anybody, and I was overwhelmed by the fact as I walked down the aisle and onto the stage. Nobody shouted or applauded. Clearly they were all waiting for the evening's attraction."[17]

With their cameras, tripods, and lights set up in front of the podium, seven or eight TV film crews were waiting in anticipation of King's arrival. Several were covering the event for the major television networks. As Abernathy would recollect: "That meant the audience would be national, so the event was much more important than a poorly attended local rally."[18] Abernathy told Jackson that he intended to telephone King and urge him to come to Mason Temple at once to speak. According to Abernathy, Jackson replied, "Don't call him. If you don't want to speak, then I'll speak."

Ignoring Jackson, Abernathy hurried to the temple vestibule where there was a telephone and called the Lorraine. King answered.

"Martin," Abernathy said, "all the television networks are lined up waiting for you. This speech will be broadcast nationwide. You need to deliver it. Besides, the people who are here want you. Not me."

"I'll do whatever you say. If you say come, I'll be there," King said. Abernathy replied, "Come."[19]

Moments later, King left the motel. He arrived at Mason Temple about nine o'clock. The crowd had been waiting an hour and a half for King. The sight of him striding toward the podium set off another deafening cacophony of shouts and applause. As the crowd's excitement washed over him, King grinned widely and took a seat on the podium.

Abernathy was no longer the main event. But he was wound up to talk. He would recall feeling an impulse, a powerful desire to exalt King's greatness to this audience on this night.[20] Abernathy offered to introduce his friend.

King and Abernathy had a friendship like no other. They had stood shoulder to shoulder during King's civil rights campaigns since the earliest days of the Montgomery bus boycott. With Abernathy bravely accompanying King as moral support and for the safety of numbers, they had gone to jail together time and again. More weeks than not, they were on the road together. They had preached in each other's churches, vacationed together, eaten in each other's homes on countless occasions, and become enmeshed in the lives of each other's families.

King's other aides, no matter how close their relationship with him, called him Martin or "Doc." Not Abernathy. For Abernathy the name was Michael. Nor did King call his friend Ralph, as others did. To each other they were Michael and David. Those were their boyhood names. Using them was a private compact between best friends, a sign of the special bond between them.

That night, during his address to the garbage workers in Mason Temple, King would express his feelings publicly for Abernathy. Once Abernathy had finished the introduction and yielded the rostrum to him, King would say: "Ralph Abernathy is the best friend that I have in the world."[21]

They were not obviously cut out to be best friends. King was the heir to the ministerial crown of his father, one of Atlanta's most esteemed African American ministers. The younger King was a highly educated scholar of theology. Abernathy was one of twelve children born to a poor cotton farmer in Marengo County, Alabama. Though he had a master's degree in sociology from Atlanta University, Abernathy, a self-described "country preacher," was not known for his erudition. As historian David Lewis summed it up, Abernathy's "intellectual pretensions were modest."[22]

That said, both were Southern-born Baptist preachers. They were roughly the same age, Abernathy being three years older. Called to serve in pulpits at two leading African American churches in Montgomery, they seemed destined either for friendship or crosstown rivalry. Close friends they became. They enjoyed each other's company and a common sense of humor. They shared a profound commitment to work together and face constant danger during their years of struggle for racial justice.

It did not seem to undercut their friendship that the chunky, sluggish Abernathy was a favorite butt of King's pranks and ribbing. King would josh him about how snoring kept him awake all night when they were in a jail cell together.[23] Once, according to an account in the *Atlanta-Journal Constitution*, King ushered Abernathy into a car that had a rusted-out floorboard with only a gaping hole for his friend's feet. Sometimes the teasing had an edge. The only organization that Ralph could lead was the "National Association for the Advancement of Eating Chicken," King once ridiculed his buddy, according to Andrew Young.[24]

If Abernathy seemed good-natured about jokes at his expense, he had his pride. At times he exhibited jealousy at all the attention showered on King. In Oslo for the Nobel Prize ceremony in King's honor, Abernathy had demanded that his wife, Juanita, and he ride in a limousine carrying Nobel Committee chairman Gunnar Jahn, King, and King's wife, Coretta. The request was denied, but Abernathy protested. According to historian Taylor Branch's account: "Abernathy appealed to King, who stood frozen with embarrassment, then tried to push his way past the security officers." Abernathy finally relented and resigned himself to riding in a car apart from Jahn and the Kings.[25]

On this night in Memphis, however, Abernathy betrayed no trace of jealousy. On the contrary, he launched into a glowing, twenty-five-minute tribute. "Brothers and sisters, ladies and gentlemen," he began, "too often we take our leaders for granted. We think we know them, but they are really strangers to us. So tonight I would like to take a little time to introduce you to our leader, Dr. Martin Luther King Jr."[26]

He went on to recite highlights of King's biography: his birth, early schooling, college years, deep involvement in the civil rights movement, and finally his plunge into the Memphis crisis on behalf of the garbage workers. "Now all you know that Martin Luther King Jr. is a great preacher," he said. "But I want you to know that he was prepared by God to be a great preacher."

Warming to the theme, Abernathy continued, "His great granddaddy was a preacher. His granddaddy was a preacher. His daddy is a preacher. His brother is a preacher, and, of course, his dearest friend and other brother . . ."—here Abernathy gestured toward himself—"is one of the world's greatest preachers. So Martin Luther King Jr. is not only a great preacher but a great leader who has the courage and ability to translate the Sermon on the Mount into lessons for our times. He's giving Mahatma Gandhi's ideas new life."[27]

In a final gush of praise that the *Commercial Appeal* would quote the next day, he said that, despite King's many honors, he was not yet seeking to be president of the United States, but "he is the man who tells the president what to do."

With applause rippling through the auditorium Abernathy paused. Then he said, "Let's give Martin Luther King a warm welcome back to Memphis." And the crowd lurched to its feet in a standing ovation.

Abernathy would say later that he had been "trying to sum up the greatness of the man in a way I had never done before."[28] After Abernathy sat down, a minister on the podium whispered to King that the introduction could have been a eulogy. King welcomed the joke with a smile.[29]

Chapter 15

From the Mountaintop

And God grant that we shall choose the high way,
even if it will mean assassination,
even if it will mean crucifixion.

—MLK, in a sermon at Dexter Avenue
Baptist Church, Montgomery, Alabama,
March 22, 1959

KING SAT QUIETLY through Abernathy's flattering introduction. Abernathy sat down, and King replaced him at the rostrum. Pausing a moment, he peered over a welter of microphones. As TV cameramen flooded him with light, his face took on a luminous sheen.

But something seemed amiss. He looked "harried and tired and worn and rushed," observed one minister.[1] He had a sore throat and was sleep-deprived. By the end of the speech that he would deliver that night, everyone in Mason Temple would know another reason why he seemed out of sorts.

As he gazed into the vastness of the auditorium, he could see hundreds of strikers and their supporters bunched together near the speaker's platform. Beyond that crowd of rapt faces, he could see the dispiriting sight of row upon row of empty seats.

Speaking slowly, softly, he thanked Abernathy for the kind introduction.

Then he greeted the audience, lauding them for braving the storm, coming to the rally, showing that they had the backbone to carry on with the strike.[2]

In the words to follow he had nothing more to say about the storm. Yet you could say that the storm still had something to say to him. Near the ceiling of the auditorium were two large window fans. They were turned off, their shutters closed. But wind gusts punched them open time and again. The shutters clacked shut each time, startling King. "Every time there was a bang, he would flinch," Billy Kyles would recall.[3]

Someone finally turned on the fans to open the shutters and stop the racket, but King had to deal with other irritations. There was the numbing exhaustion from travel and his chronic insomnia, and despair at being trapped in Memphis. Somehow he had to muster the energy and gumption to lift the spirits of this crowd, even though his were terribly low.

There had been no time to prepare, even if he had intended to do so. He often spoke without notes, even when the stakes were extremely high. He was doing it again on this night.

He had an astonishing knack for speaking off the cuff. He seemingly had a photographic memory. In his first big moment as a civil rights leader, during the kickoff rally to commence the Montgomery bus boycott in 1955, he had twenty minutes to compose his remarks.[4] He had delivered a riveting speech that had his audience clapping and howling their support. The "I have a dream" finale of his speech at the March on Washington in 1963 catapulted him to legendary heights. That stunning riff was famously a spur-of-the-moment departure from the prepared text.

The first theme of his remarks at Mason Temple that Wednesday night seemed far removed from Memphis. Imagine, he said, still speaking quietly, that the "Almighty" was transferring him back in time. King's first stop, he said, would be Egypt in biblical times. He would visit classical Greece, the Roman Empire, the Renaissance, the Christian Reformation under his namesake Martin Luther, and Lincoln's signing of the Emancipation Proclamation.[5]

King said he would not stop his trip through history there. No, he would ask the Almighty to allow him to live in current-day America.

The specifics of the trip through time, of course, were not the point of King's speech. They were a rhetorical device to lend emphasis and gravity to his words. It was the kind of flair that King employed to infuse his speeches and sermons with dramatic power. In the Memphis speech he was mixing the simplicity of a children's story, a bird's-eye view of history, with references to lofty historical figures.

Under segregation, blacks could attend the Overton Park Zoo on Thursdays. The rest of the week and holidays, the zoo was for whites only.

William Edwin Jones pushes eight-month-old daughter Renee in protest on Main Street in Memphis, August 1961.

A security guard watches garbage workers empty trash into a compressor-equipped truck, as the Memphis strike enters its third day, on February 15, 1968.

The striking garbage workers staged daily marches carrying signs stating their emotional slogan: "I Am a Man."

MLK arrives at the Memphis airport on the morning of April 3 with aides (l to r) Andrew Young, Ralph Abernathy, and Bernard Lee.

Jubilant strike leaders celebrate at the end of MLK's speech in Mason Temple on March 18, 1968.

Mason Temple offered a cavernous forum, where MLK delivered two dramatic speeches to pro-strike rallies, including this one on March 18, 1968.

Rev. Jim Lawson leads strike supporters in a boycott against downtown stores. The sign refers to Mayor Henry Loeb.

At six foot five, Mayor Henry Loeb cut a physically imposing figure. He proved to be an implacable foe of the garbage workers' strike.

MLK is jostled by an unruly crowd as he prepares to lead a march on behalf of the garbage workers, on March 28, 1968.

When he was traveling, King carried a briefcase stuffed with papers that reflected his widely varied interests, ranging from food production in the Mideast to the causes of urban rioting in the United States.

As US marshal Cato Ellis serves an injunction on MLK, King and his aides (l to r), Ralph Abernathy, Andrew Young, James Orange, and Bernard Lee, share a laugh to lighten the mood.

MLK's aide Jesse Jackson shares a private thought with him on the platform of Mason Temple during the pro-strike rally on April 3 1968.

MLK delivers his "Mountaintop" speech at Mason Temple on the evening of April 3, 1968.

Arriving in the Memphis federal courthouse on April 4, 1968, to contest an injunction against MLK was Lucius Burch, his legal team, and their witnesses. Pictured, from left, Rev. James Lawson, SCLC executive director Andrew Young, and lawyers Burch, Charles Newman, and W. J. Michael Cody.

As he imagined the stop in ancient Greece, he spoke of his expectation that he would bump into Pluto, Aristotle, Socrates, Euripides, and Aristophanes. If few of his listeners would have recognized all those names, that did not matter. King was burnishing his speech with a dash of intellectual gloss. It was not just Martin Luther King speaking. It was Dr. King, the theologian with a PhD from Boston University. It was a learned man who could rattle off the names of ancient philosophers and dramatists to poetic effect.

His voice built in intensity and rose in volume as he went on. That voice, a rich baritone, seemed to emerge from deep within him, as though rumbling from an oak barrel. His voice was almost musical in its harmonic rise and fall. It was at once lucid and richly ornate. On another occasion the timbre of that voice had bowled over the newspaper columnist Mary McGrory. Writing in the *Washington Evening Star* on December 16, 1966, she noted how "baroque phrases" slid off his tongue in "mellifluous, mesmerizing tones."

King's voice could, depending on the race or sophistication of his audience, exhibit the clipped diction of a lofty academic or the earthy vernacular of African American speech. For example, on one occasion, in 1965, when he was speaking in the vernacular, he proclaimed from the steps of the Alabama statehouse at the conclusion of a triumphant march from Selma to Montgomery: "We ain't goin' let nobody turn us around."[6]

As he moved to a major theme of his speech at Mason Temple, King turned darkly pessimistic. He said that the choice for humankind was no longer between violence and nonviolence. Tapping his fingers on the rostrum, he said the choice, rather, was between nonviolence and "nonexistence." Unless the government moved swiftly to alleviate the poverty of African Americans, he said, the nation was doomed.

It was not a momentary lapse into overstatement. King had been saying much the same thing for months. He was warning of catastrophe. Nothing less. It was why he saw poverty as an issue of overriding urgency.

King shifted to another message, a plea for unity. He urged the strikers to stick together, invoking a passage from the Old Testament. Just as the slaves of ancient Egypt united against the Pharaoh to escape their bondage, so the strikers had to stay together, united.

In a jab at the mayor he insinuated that Loeb was not just wrong to defy the strikers. He was sick, King said. King sympathized with the strikers' hardship, as they struggled to feed their families and put their livelihood at risk without knowing if their strike would succeed or fail.

To signal that victory was at hand, he recounted the familiar story of Birmingham: how his legion of protesters had withstood fire hoses, police dogs, mass arrests, and jail sentences. Just as the power of the nonviolent movement had worked in Birmingham, he said, that same spirit could win the struggle in Memphis.

Then his words took on a sharply defiant tone. He declared that neither Mace nor a court injunction would defeat the cause of the Memphis strikers. He repeated the call for an economic boycott of certain stores and products in order to exert business pressure on the mayor. Ever more animated, his right hand slashing downward, he extolled the boycott as the force that would win the day. He said it would cause downtown businesses to demand that Loeb grant the rightness of the strikers' cause.

King shifted his focus again, from the immediacy of the strike to a second biblical theme. This time he drew on the parable of the Good Samaritan to urge people who had no vested interest in the strike to support it anyway. The story, told by Jesus and recorded in the Gospel of Luke, speaks of a traveler on the dangerous Jericho Road who is robbed and beaten by thieves. A priest and a Levite pass the man as they hurry on their way. Then a Samaritan, who belonged to a different ethnic group, stopped to aid the injured man. King suggested that the priest and the Levite did not stop to help because of fear that thieves might also attack them. King said that, like the Samaritan, people in Memphis should not ask about the risk to themselves if they helped the garbage workers. No, he said, they should be thinking about the fate of the garbage workers if they did not help them.

King had preached the parable of the Good Samaritan in many of his Sunday sermons.[7] He had done so just six weeks before. Then he had added another thought. Good deeds were admirable, he said, but they were not enough. Stronger laws were essential as well.

He had a keen sense of what messages and symbols would resonate with which audience. Relying on biblical tropes was very much in tune with the makeup of the crowd at Mason Temple. Ingrained in the marrow of most everyone in that auditorium was a biblical heritage and Christian belief. Thus far into the speech he had invoked the name of God (or "Almighty") fourteen times, and he had summoned parables from the Old and New Testaments. He would refer to God twice more before he finished.

Religious motifs came naturally to him. Even when King was a small boy, his father, the Reverend Martin Luther King Sr., had him memorizing scripture and reciting it at the dinner table. His mother, a church organist, instilled a religious spirit through the power of song. Every Sunday he sat in a wooden pew of his father's church. Before his eyes were the biblically themed stained glass windows above the pulpit. Into his ears poured Gospel-laden sermons and the voices of the white-robed choir, all radiating the Christian faith and the African American Baptist tradition.

From a young age he had displayed a knack for public speaking. He was only fifteen, in his last year of high school (he skipped two grades in high school), when he won a statewide oratorical contest for African American students. When he was eighteen, his father invited him to deliver a trial Sunday-afternoon sermon at Ebenezer. Though he had no formal training in the ministry, he obliged. King biographer Taylor Branch described what happened: the novice preacher "seemed to project his entire being in the expression of his sentiments," and the worshippers "rose up in celebration."[8]

As a graduate student in theology King honed and refined his speaking style. He mastered the charismatic techniques and sermonizing of African American Baptist preachers, such as C. L. Franklin, and white clergymen Emerson Fosdick and George Buttrick. He scrutinized and memorized their mannerisms until he could do dead-on imitations. He had a repertoire of them, and years later he would amuse his aides with exaggerated renditions of one preacher's style or another.

He was alert to the possibilities of metaphor and imagery and systematic in building a stock of rhetorical material. In a brown pocket-sized spiral notebook he jotted down witticisms that caught his eye. "Nothing so educates as a shake" was one scribbling. Another was from Jean-Jacques Rousseau: "Above the logic is the feeling of the heart."[9]

Flashes of his mastery with words were on display at Mason Temple that Wednesday night. As he often did in his speeches, he elevated a local issue into a sweeping, transcendent national cause. He implored his listeners to support the garbage workers of Memphis. By doing so, he said, they would not just shape their city's future; they would also transform the nation with their example.

Then his speech took a highly personal turn. He told of being stabbed in 1958 by a crazed African American woman while he was signing books in Harlem. The tip of the blade lodged in his chest a fraction of an inch from his aorta. Surgery removed the knife and repaired the wound. He later learned that he had been extremely lucky. If he had so much as sneezed while the knife impinged on the artery, he would have died. He told of receiving a letter from an eleven-year-old girl. King quoted from the letter in which the girl said she was glad that he had not sneezed.

The story of the stabbing and the girl's letter served as a rhetorical lead-in for a recap of his career. "If I had sneezed," he sang out over and over in a melodic refrain, each time citing a key event in the civil rights movement that he would have missed had he died from the stabbing in Harlem. If he had sneezed, he said, he would have missed the sit-in protests to desegregate lunch counters. If he had sneezed, he would have missed the Freedom Rides to end Jim Crow on interstate buses, the Birmingham campaign, the enactment of the federal civil rights bills, the chance to deliver the "I Have a Dream" speech in Washington, the showdown in Selma over voting rights, and the outpouring of community support in Memphis for the strike that had brought him there.

Reciting the story about his near death seemed to transport him into a profound gloom about mortality—his mortality. Still fresh on his mind was the death threat that forced the delay of his flight from Atlanta that morning, and he could not let it go now. He told his listeners how the airline had taken the threat seriously because he was on board, had guarded the plane during the night and checked all the passengers' bags for explosives. Upon his arrival in Memphis, King said, he had heard yet more talk about death threats against him.

He continued in a melancholy, self-reflective mood, saying he was facing some difficult days ahead. But he said he was prepared for anything, no matter what might lay ahead, because he had "been to the Mountaintop."[10]

His words reflected a soul searching as he contemplated the specter of death. He had talked many times before about his fear of dying a violent death. But it was unusual for King to dwell openly on the depth of his despair as he pondered his fear of death. His manner typically was light-hearted, self-assured, and unflappable. This night in Memphis, however, he seemed near panic, anxious that he might be the target of an assassin's bullet at any moment.

For many years he had dealt openly with that fear. During his earliest civil rights leadership, in Montgomery, his front porch had been bombed. He proclaimed defiantly at a rally soon afterward: "Tell Montgomery that they can keep bombing, and I'm going to stand up to them. If I had to die tomorrow morning, I would die happy because I've been to the Mountaintop, and I've seen the Promised Land, and it's going to be here in Montgomery."[11] In other speeches, memorably in Demopolis, Alabama, during the Selma-to-Montgomery march of 1965, he had spoken about his fear that he might be killed. For years he felt a gnawing doubt that he would live to the age of forty. "I'll never live to be forty. I'll never make it," he told his lawyer, Chauncey Eskridge.[12]

By early 1968, as he entered his fortieth year, the fear was seizing him with fierce intensity. In a Sunday sermon on February 4 at Ebenezer, he dwelled on the prospect of his early death, effectively preaching his own eulogy. No need to catalog all the honors bestowed on him, he said. Rather, he said, "I'd like somebody to mention that day that Martin Luther King, Jr., tried to give his life serving others . . . [that he] was a drum major for justice."[13]

Not long after, on March 12, he sent synthetic red carnations to his wife. Until then all the flowers he had ever given her had been real. In justifying his choice of flowers, he told Coretta: "I wanted to give you something that you could always keep."[14] In late March, as he girded himself for the return to Memphis, he confided to his parents that they ought to brace for his death at any time.[15]

Now, as he concluded his speech at Mason Temple, he seemed to be coming to terms with death to an extent that he had not voiced publicly before.

His voice rose to its highest pitch yet. His eyes blinked rapidly, as he turned his head from side to side. He acknowledged that he wanted to live a long life but that he was resigned to whatever might happen. He said that God had allowed him to reach the mountaintop and see the Promised Land. Then he vowed resolutely, nobly: "I may not get there with you. But I want you to know, tonight, that we, as a people, will *get* to the Promised Land!"

He ended with an utterance of religious fervor, saying that he was not worried, that he did not fear anybody, exclaiming in a final flourish, "Mine eyes have seen the glory of the coming of the Lord."

That borrowing from the "Battle Hymn of the Republic" was a staple of his oratory. The words, penned by Julia Ward Howe in 1861, venerate a fierce fight to the death in the name of freedom for American slaves. It is a call to abolitionists to follow Jesus in sacrificing themselves for a righteous cause. If King had completed the stanza, he would have added: "The truth is marching on." But he did not. His wife, Coretta, reading his words spoken at Mason Temple, would think that he had become so overcome by emotion that he could not finish the stanza.[16]

Coming to terms with the prospect of his death and his own sacrifice, King was approaching grandiosity. He was comparing himself to Jesus and Moses—to the Jesus heralded in the "Battle Hymn" and to the Old Testament's celebration of the Moses who had led his people toward the Promised Land.

Other speeches had drawn the parallel between the civil rights movement and the Exodus story. Now he was adding a new element. As Moses was to the Israelites' struggle for freedom, he seemed to be saying, he was to African Americans' struggle for freedom. As he stared at the face of death, he was portraying himself as the Moses of his time.

He had talked for forty-three minutes. Spent by the exertion, tears welling in his eyes, he turned and staggered toward his chair on the podium. Wobbly, he seemed to lose his footing. Ralph Abernathy caught him and steered him into the chair. "It was as though somebody had taken a beach ball and pulled the plug out, as if all his energy had been sucked out," the lawyer Mike Cody recalled.[17]

As King collapsed into his chair, the crowd rose up from theirs, roaring and clapping. Historian Joan Beifuss would describe the crowd as "caught between tears and applause."[18]

Even among the ministers in the auditorium who knew King's oratory well, the emotional charge of his words provoked shivers. "I'd never heard the intensity or the passion or the drama in his voice, in how he was delivering it, and he kept getting stronger and stronger," Billy Kyles would say.[19] He would add that King seemed to be preparing for his death by purging publicly "the fear. He had to get rid of it. He had to let all that go." Abernathy would write in his memoir: "I had heard him hit high notes before, but never any higher."[20] Jesse Jackson would call his wife to tell her "Martin had given the most brilliant speech of his life [and say] that he was lifted up and had some mysterious aura around him."[21] Years later, Jackson would note: "What I thought was so different about that sermon, I saw men crying," not something that happens usually in church.[22] By the end, Kyles would say, "We were on our feet clapping and hollering."[23]

As often happened at the end of a compelling speech by King, the crowd surged toward him. Rather than allow a crowd to crush him, he usually exited quickly. "But that night he just didn't want to leave," Beifuss would quote a local minister as saying. "He just wanted to stay there and meet people and shake their hands and talk to them."[24] It was not an ordinary night.

Chapter 16

Long Night

*I just want to spend a quiet evening here with you
without worrying about the problems that beset me.*

—MLK, comment to Georgia Davis,
Chicago, spring of 1967

BY THE END OF HIS SPEECH at Mason Temple, King was wrung out—
not just physically but also emotionally. Yet, despite his fatigue and the
wrenching drama of the evening, he was in a better frame of mind than he
had been earlier in the day. The crowd's jubilant reception seemed to dispel
the gloom that had enveloped him.[1]

There likely was another reason for his brighter spirits. He was expecting Kentucky state senator Georgia Davis, with whom he was having an
affair, to arrive at the Lorraine that night. Davis was driving to Memphis from Florida, along with King's younger brother, A.D., and another
woman, Lukey Ward.

Rather than return to his room at the Lorraine right away, King headed
to a Memphis house for a late-night dinner. Bernard Lee and Ralph Abernathy went with him. The host was a friend of King's, according to a
memoir that Abernathy published years later. Abernathy did not identify
the friend, except to say that she was a woman and a Memphian. The
friend served steak and provided dinner partners, two other women, for
Lee and Abernathy.[2]

Following the meal the three men and three women sat in the living
room of the house engaging in light conversation. Then, in Abernathy's
account, he and Lee dozed off in the living room, and King and the friend

retired to another part of the house. It was long past midnight when King reappeared. The three men departed, taking a taxi through the incessant rain back to the Lorraine.[3]

On arriving at the motel's parking lot, King saw a pink Cadillac convertible bearing Kentucky license plates. He recognized the car as Lukey Ward's. Despite the lateness of the hour, the lights were still burning brightly in A.D.'s room, 207, and in Davis's, 201. King exited the taxi and knocked on the door of Room 207. He found Davis, Ward, and his brother in the room.[4] They were still awake, restored to life by coffee.

A few days before, while in Florida, Davis had the idea that she ought to join King in Memphis. After completing a hectic session of the Kentucky legislature, she was on a sun-and-surf vacation at Fort Walton Beach. Ward, a friend of hers and fellow civil rights activist, was with her there. From TV news Davis had learned of the rioting in Memphis on March 28.

Stunned that the march being led by King had turned violent and concerned about King, Davis called the SCLC office in Atlanta. She did not reach him but left a message. When he returned the call, she told him that she was in Florida on vacation. "Are you getting a tan?" he teased, laughing.

Next he asked, "Senator, why don't you come help me?"[5]

"Well," she would recall replying, "I was thinking I've had about enough sun. I will be there Tuesday or Wednesday."[6]

King's brother, A.D., was then about to leave Louisville, where he was pastor at Zion Baptist Church, to join Davis and Ward in Fort Walton Beach. He intended to spend a few days with Ward. He was planning to fly back to Louisville afterward. But King called A.D. in Louisville, saying he needed his brother's moral support in Memphis. A.D. agreed to come to Tennessee, but first he flew to Florida, arriving on Monday, April 1. Ward agreed to deliver A.D. and Davis to Memphis in her Cadillac. Early Wednesday morning, the threesome set out on the five-hundred-mile journey from Fort Walton Beach to Memphis.

Davis had blocked out a month for sun and relaxation in Florida. Heeding King's appeal for help, she had left Florida two weeks early. She felt that he needed her, that she could bolster his spirits as he faced the crisis in Memphis. Further, she would write in her memoir, she "felt guilty relaxing when so much needed to be done in the civil rights struggle."[7]

Nothing in Davis's early life foreshadowed her future as one of the "real heroes," as Kentucky governor Edward Breathitt would put it one day, of the civil rights movement in her state.[8] She was born in a two-room cabin in the farming hamlet of Jimtown (short for Jim Crow Town) in central Kentucky. Her parents, Frances and Ben Montgomery, were just teenagers when they married. Frances was fifteen, Ben nineteen. Davis was the second oldest of the nine children they would have, and the only daughter.

When she was seventeen months old, a tornado had ripped through their cabin. It might have killed her had not the mattress on her bed flipped and shielded her. Their house in ruins, the family sought refuge with relatives in Louisville. Her father landed a steady job in a foundry, and the family settled in Louisville and stayed.

They managed well enough by the standard of the African American community of Louisville. They owned their house on Grand Avenue. (Muhammad Ali would eventually live two doors down.) Davis's family always had food on the table. But her parents did not have the money to pay for their children's college. Upon graduating from Central High School, Davis swore that one way or another she would go to college. She was barred from the University of Louisville, her first choice, because of her race. It was an affront she would never forget. "How we were discriminated against and segregated," she would remember, "it put fire in my belly to make changes."[9]

She landed a two-year scholarship to attend all-black Louisville Municipal College but dropped out in her second year for lack of money. She married a man who promised to pay her tuition. He reneged, and they quickly divorced. She worked in a variety of jobs, including airplane riveter, sewing-machine operator, and data processor. She remarried, but the relationship with her second husband, a soldier, was often rocky.

Politics came to her rather than the other way around. In 1962, when she was thirty-eight, Louisville mayor Wilson Wyatt recruited her to help with clerical duties in his campaign for governor. She could neither type nor take shorthand well, but Wyatt hired her anyway. In her memoir she would note that she entered politics as the Wyatt campaign's "token black" to broaden his appeal to African American voters.[10] Wyatt lost the election anyhow.

Davis emerged from the Wyatt campaign with an itch for more politics. Over the next few years she worked on campaigns to elect Democratic candidates for governor and mayor. She gained a reputation as a crack political operative, with a savvy that she applied next to the state's civil rights movement. As head of an advocacy group in Kentucky, the Allied Organization for Civil Rights, she organized protests and lobbied lawmakers to combat racial segregation.

It was Davis's work as a civil rights activist that led her to King. They did not meet until 1964. Like many Americans, she had become aware of him during the Montgomery bus boycott. She had seen him on television and admired him greatly. Hearing him talk, identifying with his commitment, she perceived a deep connection to her own feelings and convictions.

In March 1964, King came to Kentucky to lead a march and speak at a rally in Frankfort, the state capital. Davis was an organizer of the event to build support for a desegregation bill before the legislature. Baseball legend Jackie Robinson was the other speaker.

Davis and her brother, a funeral home director, met King at the airport. She would recall: "My heart quickened as I saw him move toward us. The first thing I noticed was his small stature. I was surprised. From his image on television or perhaps the one in my own mind, I had envisioned him being taller. His skin was a mahogany brown, and he wore a trimmed mustache above his full, shapely lips. His dark brown eyes looked straight into those of whomever he was addressing."[11]

King and Davis rode in her brother's black funeral limousine to the capital building. On the way Davis briefed King about the pending civil rights bill and the plan for the day's march and rally. He commended the plan, saying that the key to civil rights progress was a strategy of mass protests and economic boycotts. She would remember being struck by the "clarity of his words and thoughts."[12]

In March 1967, King was back in Louisville for an SCLC board meeting. By then Davis had become acquainted with King's brother A.D., through her civil rights activity. Davis, who was then separated from her second husband, was working as a volunteer with a local civil rights group, the Kentucky Leadership Conference, which operated under the auspices of A.D.'s church.

Without explaining why, A.D. asked Davis to come to his office at the church. "Martin has been thinking about you and wants to meet you at the Rodeway Inn," she would remember A.D. saying to her.[13] She replied, "I'll think about it."

She slept with King that night. They would be together several more times. He sent her an airline ticket to join him while he was attending meetings in Chicago. They stayed in an apartment.[14] He and Abernathy spent a night at her house in Louisville in May 1967. It was during the Kentucky

Derby, when the hotels of Louisville were booked. She asked him to speak to a voter registration rally at the Green Baptist Church on August 3, 1967. He agreed. They were together in Louisville again at that time.[15]

Years later, when she puzzled over why she had become his lover, she would admit to herself that she was not physically attracted to him. "He just wasn't my type," she would say.[16] She would say that she enjoyed his company, that he was charming and funny, full of jokes. He would mimic other preachers to hilarious effect. He seemed joyful and relaxed with her.[17] She was flattered by his interest in her. She would put it this way: "I was middle-aged and not feeling very attractive when Martin Luther King, the leader of the civil rights movement, the man who fought so valiantly to make the dream of all black people a reality, wanted to be with me."[18]

That King would have found her attractive, despite her feeling otherwise, was not surprising. Short, bright-eyed, shapely (she would describe herself as having a "full chest"), she had a winsome smile, a gentle, lilting voice, and a mirthful cackle of a laugh.[19] From her King sought a soothing companion, and she must have satisfied that need. "He wanted compassion," she would say. "He wanted to be cuddled."[20]

Yet they retained a certain formality in their manner toward each other. Many of King's close friends called him Martin or M.L., but she always addressed him as Dr. King. To honor her request, he autographed a copy of his book *Where Do We Go from Here*. In the inscription he wrote: "To my friend, Georgia Davis, for whom I have great respect and admiration, Martin Luther King, Jr." When she looked back to her time with him, she would not think of it so much as a love affair but rather as a warm friendship between two people who were fond of each other.

Over the years, King turned to her as a lifeline to help his brother. The two brothers were close. A.D., who was seventeen months younger than King, had been best man at his wedding. But unlike his older brother, A.D. was a troubled soul. He had bowed to his father's wishes that he become a preacher but did not find it much to his liking. Davis thought that A.D. had a low opinion of himself, an inferiority complex, which she attributed to his living in the shadow of a renowned brother.[21] A.D. suffered from chronic alcoholism. When he was on a bender, he would drift into sordid nightspots where a Baptist preacher had no business going.

On more than one occasion King called Davis to say that his brother was so despondent that he was threatening suicide. King would ask her to intervene and help sober him up. She would hurry to A.D.'s house. His wife, Naomi, would let her in. Davis would find A.D. in a bedroom and ask what was wrong. Davis would recall how she would scold him. She would ask, "Why would you put that burden on your brother with all the problems he has?"[22] A.D. would reply that he was really okay, and she should not worry: he was not going to kill himself. But the brother's alcoholic binges were a continual source of worry to King.

In 1967 Davis hit upon a bold idea. Instead of working to elect another candidate for public office, she would work to elect herself. She jumped into the race for the Kentucky Senate. It seemed very much a long shot. No African American or woman had ever been elected a Kentucky state senator. In her district, whites outnumbered blacks by almost two to one. She had the guts to run anyhow, and she won.

She had served only three months in office when she arrived in Memphis in the early morning of April 4. Having found A.D., Ward, and Davis awake and in a talkative mood, King sat down with them in Room 207. King and his brother were in lighthearted spirits. They rattled off a round of jokes. The room filled with laughter.[23]

Not all of the chatter was lighthearted. The new arrivals had questions for King. What about the violence that had erupted during the march six days earlier? As Davis would recount, King said that he was concerned, that "they had rushed him out of the area, and what would people say [about his courage and leadership]?"[24] King was being pilloried in the press for having left the scene of the riot, even though the full story should have noted that he had done so under instructions from the police.

Even on the dreary subject of the riot, King could not resist a droll bit of understatement. He turned to Davis. "I would rather have been in Florida getting a tan than here in the middle of turmoil," he said.

"You are invited," she said.

He replied that there was a more urgent task for him at the moment. The Invaders had disrupted the last march, he said, and might do the same during the next one. King was determined that they would not. Davis replied, playfully, as she would recount in her memoir: "Maybe they should be called the Disrupters."[25]

There was talk of Judge Brown's injunction. King said he was directing his lawyer, Chauncey Eskridge, and Andrew Young to appear in Brown's court later that morning and urge the judge to vacate his order barring him from marching.

The conversation in Room 207 continued into the early morning. It ended when King announced that he had set a meeting with his staff for eight o'clock that morning, and he needed rest. Davis left A.D.'s room to walk toward hers. She heard King's footsteps behind her.

She left the door to her room slightly ajar, and he followed a moment later. He may have been a night owl of great stamina, but he had reached his limit. As Davis would write in her memoir: "He declared, softly, 'I've never been more physically and emotionally tired.'"

He collapsed into bed, saying, "Senator, our time together is so short." It was 4:30 a.m.

Chapter 17

Home Pressures

I'm away two and three weeks at a time. . . .
But every day when I'm at home, I break from the office
for dinner and try to spend a few hours with the children
before I return to the office for some night work.

—MLK, interview with *Playboy* magazine,
January 1965

OPERATING ON LESS than four hours sleep, King was up by 8 a.m. to face the day. Time was short before the march on Monday. Still hanging over him was the federal injunction barring him from marching. A hearing on the injunction was set for 9:30 that morning before Judge Brown. But King, the central defendant in the case, would not be going to court. He was weary from lack of sleep. Andrew Young and James Lawson would be testifying in his stead.

There were other issues that demanded his attention. One was a delicate matter involving Dorothy Cotton. She was one of his most valued aides, the only woman on his staff in an executive role. He had agreed to meet her for a bite to eat after the rally at Mason Temple the night before, but he had not shown up.[1] She would want an explanation.

It was yet another headache for King, this one self-inflicted. The Memphis crisis had all but shattered his nerves. In his fraught condition he needed the support of people close to him. His wife, Coretta (whom he called Corrie), had been at his side in troubling times. The night before, he had called her. They had talked while he was still in his room at the Lorraine before he departed for the rally at Mason Temple.

As Coretta would write in her memoir, *My Life with Martin Luther King, Jr.*, King had sounded upbeat.[2] He spoke optimistically about the prospects for a large turnout of marchers on Monday. King, however, was not entirely reassuring. The subject of Judge Brown's injunction came up. Repeating what he had indicated to others in his inner circle, King told Coretta that he would lead the march on Monday even if he had to violate the injunction.

Though King and his wife were in touch by phone, she was at home in Atlanta, not with him as he confronted the crisis in Memphis. He had summoned Georgia Davis and his brother to Memphis. It's unlikely that King had asked Coretta to come. She was recovering from surgery for a fibroid stomach tumor and not in the best shape to travel.[3]

Probably he would not have urged Coretta to come to Memphis even if she had been in perfect health. In keeping with the social convention of the times he believed a wife belonged at home caring for the children. He was always forthright about this. In proposing that they marry, he had specified that she must play the role of a traditional, stay-at-home wife attending to his needs.[4]

She agreed to marry him all the same. She had scuttled her career as a singer and music teacher to become a preacher's wife. Rather than devote herself to a career, she agreed to devote herself to him and, when the time came, to their children. So it was that she became a dutiful wife and mother. Years later, she would describe herself as having been his "confidante" and "best friend." She would say they could "finish each other's sentences," and "feel each other's wounds."[5]

For his part, he would extol her as a loyal wife to whom he was grateful for "not hampering his movement activities."[6] The tribute was incomplete. She had done more to support his activism than not stand in his way. They had comforted each other and steeled each other in the darkest hours. When their house in Montgomery was bombed, after his near death from the knife attack in Harlem, during the years of interminable telephone calls to their house from people threatening to kill him, through the travail of his many jail sentences—she was his emotional rock.

That was not all Coretta had done. In one notable coup, in 1960, she had telephoned John Kennedy, who was then the Democratic nominee for president, and prevailed on him to help free her husband from the racially toxic confines of the Georgia State Prison at Reidsville, which Kennedy had done. She had spoken to large crowds, as she did at the end of the Selma-to-Montgomery march. She had sung at fund-raising concerts to prop up the sagging treasury of the SCLC. She had always been there for him and his cause—their cause. All the same, she had played essentially an auxil-iary role.

As a young woman she had seemed more likely destined for civil rights activism than King had been in his youth. She had endured greater racist outrages. She was born in a crude, two-room house that her father had built with his own hands. She grew up in virulently racist Perry County, Alabama. (In the nearby town of Marion, in 1958, a jury sentenced a black man, Jimmy Wilson, to death for stealing $1.95 from a local woman. It took an international outcry, compelling a governor's clemency, to spare the condemned man from the electric chair.) Her entrepreneurial father had angered whites by defying a tacit rule: transporting logs as a business was only for whites. Coretta's father had nevertheless hauled logs in his truck to the local train station. White racists struck back. When she was fifteen, they had torched her family's house, leaving behind only charred embers.[7]

King had grown up in the urban, African American Old Fourth Ward of Atlanta. His had been a life cocooned from the extremes of Perry County bigotry. King would tease Coretta about her humble origins. He would say that if she had not found him, she might be back in the hot Georgia sun picking cotton.[8]

When she won a scholarship to attend Antioch College at Yellow Springs, Ohio, she received a ticket out of the South. At Antioch she stretched herself politically as a member of the campus NAACP chapter, Race Relations Committee, and Civil Liberties Committee. She clam-ored for peace at campus rallies and attended a Progressive Party conven-tion in Philadelphia.[9]

King's four years as an undergraduate at Morehouse College were very different. He signed up for the NAACP chapter, but that was as far as his political activism went.[10]

In accepting King's marital terms, Coretta ceded much of her political latitude to his control. But she never fully resigned herself to that constraint. She urged him repeatedly to allow her a larger role in the movement. She longed to be in the front line of protest. He had forbidden it. Concern for her safety was an issue. He did not want the two of them traveling and demonstrating together at the risk of orphaning their children.[11]

According to historian Adam Fairclough, she had had "virtually no part" at the SCLC, even though she had begged for a greater involvement in the movement.[12] With rare exceptions King had barred her from being with him during his civil rights campaigns. He forbid her from joining in protests, marching in racially tense cities or risking arrest and jail. He told her, "You see, I am called [by God], and you aren't."[13]

As her friend Ella Baker would put it, Coretta's gender, not just motherhood, had excluded her from playing a significant role at the SCLC. Baker urged her to seek a greater role, to demand a seat among the "councils of men."[14]

Baker had been the first executive director of the SCLC. She held that position from 1957 to 1960 but left the organization after a falling-out with King. In her place King installed a man, Wyatt Walker. A personality clash with King may have been part of the reason.[15] But Baker saw King's desire to push her aside as a sexist act. Dorothy Cotton agreed. She would note that "sexist attitudes" within the SCLC meant that "men were the leaders and women were the followers and supporters."[16]

Sexism pervaded the whole of the civil rights movement, not only at the SCLC. Stokely Carmichael, referring to his own organization, the Student Nonviolent Coordinating Committee, had made the point jocularly, yet notoriously and revealingly: "The position of women in SNCC is prone," he had said.[17]

Coretta saw herself as victimized by the sexist mind-set of the time. She groused to him about it but to little effect. Her discontent festered between them, a sore that wouldn't heal.

That was not the only source of marital friction between them. Sometimes she felt like a single mother, and she shared her frustration with King.[18] As a rule, King was away three weeks of every four.[19] Even when he was at home, he was often too busy for a normal life. In 1960, Coretta complained to an interviewer for *Life* magazine: "We like to read and listen to music, but we don't have time for it. We can't even sit down to supper without somebody coming to the door."[20]

King was on the road when two of their children, Marty and Dexter, had their tonsils removed. Preoccupied by his travel commitments, he did not call home to ask how the surgery had gone.[21] Nor was he around much to help Coretta recuperate after the births of each of their four children.[22] In years to come she would say that she had yielded to his being absent so much for the greater cause of civil rights. But she admitted, wistfully, her regret at having been deprived a full family life.

Then there was the constant tension over money and the lack of it to buy what she thought they should have. King was a natty dresser but otherwise stuck to a Gandhi-like vow to live plainly. As an advocate for the downtrodden, King thought he should own as little as possible. He wanted few possessions. His cramped, cluttered office at SCLC headquarters on Auburn Street in Atlanta reflected his lack of interest in material trappings. A reporter for the *Baltimore Sun* visited King in the office in June 1965. He described it as having "dingy green walls and a bare floor." King sat in a creaky swivel chair behind an old wooden desk.

Had he not denounced riches, he could have been a wealthy man. Honoraria from his speaking engagements poured in at the rate of $200,000 or more a year. But he kept only a tiny fraction for himself. The rest he diverted to the SCLC treasury. He allowed himself an income of $10,000 to $12,000 a year: $4,000 from Ebenezer Church, $2,000 in parsonage allowance, and at most $6,000 in speaker's fees that he retained for himself. He accepted only a one-dollar annual salary from the SCLC (qualifying his family for a group insurance plan). In spite of Coretta's strong objection, he donated all of his $54,000 in Nobel Prize money to the movement. She had pleaded with him, vainly, to set aside $20,000 to start a fund for their children's education.[23]

Ultimately, he did bow to Coretta's repeated demands that they own a house rather than rent. In 1965 they bought a modest bungalow on Sunset Street in the lower-middle-class Vine City neighborhood of Atlanta. The house had a two-car garage. But the Kings had just one car, a 1960 Ford, to park in it.

Reports of King's marital infidelity threatened to fray his relations with Coretta all the more. How much she knew of the allegations is not clear. There is no evidence that she was aware of his affair with Georgia Davis, much less that he had invited her to Memphis.

Had Davis been his only lover outside marriage, he more easily could have kept Coretta in the dark. But there were others, according to various accounts. In his memoir Abernathy acknowledged King's (and his own) "extramarital relations."[24] King's two most authoritative biographers, Taylor

Branch and David Garrow, claim that King had longtime mistresses, whom they don't name, in Atlanta and Los Angeles.[25]

That many women took a fancy to her husband was no surprise to Coretta. It didn't hurt that he was funny and charming. His effect on women was magnetic and powerful for another reason. In the eyes of some women he was a hero, an eloquent, courageous fighter for African Americans. In her memoir Coretta would quote him, tellingly, as having described women as "hero-worshipers."[26] If hints about her husband's extramarital dalliances reached Coretta's ears, she blanked them out. Or so she said, and Abernathy agreed. He would write, "She rose above all the petty attempts to damage their marriage by refusing to even entertain such thoughts."[27] The thoughts might have entered her head anyhow. Without admitting knowledge of King's philandering, Coretta artfully evaded the issue. As quoted by Garrow, she stated: "If I ever had suspicions . . . I never would have even mentioned them to Martin. I just wouldn't have burdened him with anything so trivial."[28]

Certainly, she could not have been entirely clueless. As far back as 1957, the rumor circulated in Montgomery that he was unfaithful to his wife. That year, the black-owned *Pittsburgh Courier* newspaper printed a gossipy blurb saying that "a prominent minister in the Deep South, a man who has been making the headlines recently in his fight for civil rights" risked creating a scandal by being caught "in a hotel room with a woman other than his wife." The man's identity, though undisclosed, was obvious to many in civil rights circles.[29]

Years later, an audiotape revealing King's sexual conduct at the Willard Hotel in Washington, DC, in 1964, with a woman other than his wife wound up in Coretta's hands. The tape was the twisted handiwork of the FBI as part of the bureau's secret, multiyear bugging operation against King. It began as a misguided investigation of King as a communist. It had mutated into an illegal, runaway smear campaign to damage King's reputation and blackmail him into quitting the movement. FBI director J. Edgar Hoover had ordered the tape sent anonymously to the SCLC headquarters in Atlanta.[30] Without listening to it, a staff member had forwarded it on to the Kings' house. Coretta had listened, along with her husband. Later she declared that she could not identify the man caught on the tape as King.[31]

If doubts about King's fidelity caused her lasting heartache, she did not admit as much in her memoir. The tone was overwhelmingly reverential toward her husband. In a ghostwritten autobiography based on interviews with her and published in 2017, eleven years after her death, she is quoted as having stated that she did not have a single "instance of proof of Martin's infidelity."[32]

But whatever the extent of his wife's knowledge of King's extramarital relations, he could not avoid self-reproach. The guilt about his being a "sinner," as he would put it, appeared to be causing him great distress by the winter of 1968. As a matter of religious principle, he subscribed to the biblical prohibition against sex outside marriage.[33] In a sermon at Ebenezer on March 4 his feelings gushed forth in self-condemnation, though he left the details to the congregation's imagination. The sermon, based on a biblical passage about King David of Israel not fulfilling his dream of building a temple in Jerusalem, dealt with the regret that comes from falling short of one's standards. He told his parishioners that they need not "go out this morning saying that Martin Luther King is a saint" but rather that he was a "sinner like all of God's children."[34]

The gnawing guilt over his sinful lapses, along with the marital tensions in his life, only added to the strain on him as he confronted the crisis in Memphis. According to David Garrow, some of King's aides saw King's marital troubles as an important factor contributing to the depths of despair into which he sank after the rioting in the Tennessee city.[35]

Chapter 18

Invaders' Exit

*It would be an act of romantic illusions for the
Negro to feel that he can win a violent revolution.*

—MLK, speaking at an SCLC retreat in Atlanta,
January 15, 1968

THE INVADERS WERE ON King's mind as he dragged himself out of bed
on Thursday morning. He struggled to his feet for a brief meeting with
his staff.

His aides reported back that their meetings with the Invaders the day
before had not produced a clear-cut pledge from the Black Power group to
cooperate with King on terms that were acceptable to him. The Invaders
were still pressing hard for money as a condition of their support, and they
were not clearly disavowing violence.

The haggling seemed nonstop. King's patience was wearing thin, his
trust in the Black Power group ebbing.[1] He asked his staff to redouble their
efforts to bring the Invaders around. Still weary from too little sleep, he
returned to bed for more rest.[2]

Refreshed by the catnap, King left his room to look for Dorothy Cotton.
A deeply committed civil rights activist, she was an integral part of his staff
in Atlanta. And in Memphis, she had a key role to play.

Cotton was thirty-eight, a year younger than King. Round-cheeked and
bright-eyed, quick to laugh, she favored stylish dresses and dangling ear-
rings. She had grown up poor in segregated Goldsboro, North Carolina.
Working to pay her way, she earned an undergraduate degree at Virginia

State College in Petersburg, Virginia, and a master's degree in education from Boston University.

She joined the SCLC staff in 1960 and threw herself heart and soul into the movement. She relocated to Atlanta, leaving her husband of five years, George Cotton, behind in Petersburg.

King asked her to head educational programs at the SCLC. Her specialty was training civil rights activists in the philosophy and methods of nonviolent protest. In that role she helped to organize workshops that trained the members of the so-called Children's Crusade, the young people who took to the streets during the Birmingham campaign in 1963.

Now King intended to repeat the strategy of Birmingham, at least to the extent that time allowed, in Memphis. He was relying on Cotton to organize workshops in Memphis that would train people in nonviolence. But she had less than a week to do in Tennessee what it had taken many weeks to accomplish in Alabama. Recruiting the Invaders was a central part of King's strategy. He was asking the Invaders to cooperate with the SCLC in endorsing nonviolence and helping to build "a larger coalition across the city," as Cotton would put it years later.[3]

On that Thursday morning, King found Cotton in her room at the Lorraine. She was seething from his not having met her for a snack the night before, as they had agreed. Now she confronted him. They argued.[4] Furious, she told him she was leaving for the airport to catch a plane back to Atlanta. "Get a later plane," she would quote him as saying. She left anyway. In Cotton's memoir, published decades later, she said that she had left Memphis to attend a meeting in Atlanta.[5]

Lawyers and witnesses, meanwhile, were convening at the US District Court in downtown Memphis for a hearing on Judge Brown's injunction. If Brown did not vacate the order before Monday and King stuck to his vow to march anyway, the judge was likely to find him in contempt. King could wind up in jail. To jail him and prevent him from marching would escalate the already heated racial tensions in Memphis.

The hearing opened with the testimony of Frank Holloman. "I am convinced that Dr. Martin Luther King, his leaders or any others cannot control a massive march of this kind in this city or elsewhere," the police director stated.[6] He went on, "I fear for the lives and property of the citizens of Memphis during the march."

When it was the turn of Andrew Young and James Lawson to testify later that day, they would reassure the judge that King and his aides meant to keep the march orderly and nonviolent. Their lawyer, Lucius Burch, urged the judge to allow the march to proceed under King's guidance. Surely, he argued, violence would be less likely to erupt with King in charge than if thousands were to march without him.

Back at the Lorraine, meanwhile, King's aides were resuming negotiations with the Invaders. The Black Power group included Charles Cabbage and a half dozen others. In the SCLC delegation were Bevel, Williams, Orange, and Lee.

A FBI field report, drawing on the observations of undercover police officer Marrell McCollough, who was in the meeting, would describe what happened. The lanky Cabbage did most of the talking in his sonorous drawl. He repeated the group's willingness to serve as parade marshals. But he reiterated their seemingly nonnegotiable condition: the SCLC must first agree to fund the Invaders' community programs. Andrew Young would recall hearing of the Invaders' demands: "They wanted us to buy their support. They were talking about our giving them a million dollars to buy cars and things. I said, 'Look, we don't have a million dollars to run our whole organization, see?' At that time we were running the organization on about half a million dollars a year."[7]

With the talks seemingly stalled, King ducked into the meeting. Cabbage still seemed far from embracing definitively the principle of nonviolence. Rather, he professed support for "tactical" violence. In Black Power terms "tactical" violence meant Watts-type rioting for the purpose of drawing urgent attention to racial grievances. King replied that either the Invaders were for nonviolence or they were not. There was no in-between. His frustration mounting, he added, "I don't negotiate with brothers."[8] The meeting ended with the prospect of the Invaders' cooperation ever more in doubt.

King and Abernathy were back in their room by noon. King, having skipped breakfast again, wanted an early lunch. He and Abernathy headed to the dining room of the Lorraine. When they were seated, a waitress told them that the day's special was catfish. That must have been very welcome news. The catfish that they had eaten on earlier visits was one of their fondest memories of the motel. At the Lorraine the fish was served Southern style: deep fried to a crispy, golden brown.

Southern style was exactly what King wanted. He craved not just fried catfish. He craved the whole gamut of Southern food. He relished everything from hominy grits to corn bread to turnip greens to barbecued pork ribs. A favorite lunch was a pork chop sandwich. At times he liked nothing better than gnawing on a pig's foot. His good friend Benjamin Hooks would say that soul food had a peculiar value in the black civil rights movement. Dinners prepared by the ministers' wives were memorable events. Hooks explained it this way: "The tension of the marches. The threats on your daily life. The uncertainty of everything. The injustice you had to face. Dinner was an outlet. You could look forward to the best cooking."[9]

This Thursday, their nerves on edge because of the crisis in Memphis, King and Abernathy were having lunch by themselves. They told the waitress they each wanted the day's special with iced tea. They waited for what seemed like an eternity. When the waitress returned to their table, she was carrying a tray. On it were not two plates of catfish but one. It was a double order heaped on one plate At least one part of the order was right: there were two glasses of iced tea on the tray.

Abernathy eyed the single plate of catfish warily. "I opened my mouth to say something," he would recall, "but Martin raised his hand." As Abernathy reconstructed the conversation years later, King said: "Oh, Ralph. Don't bother her anymore. She probably doesn't get paid minimum wage, and you know what the tips must be like here. We'll just eat from the same plate." And they did.[10]

In the early afternoon King convened another meeting of his staff. He was fuming about how the Invaders were dealing with him. He was insisting on a total pledge of nonviolence, which they were withholding as they angled for a million-dollar funding commitment. Some of his aides reminded him that the Invaders had leverage. Unless the Invaders got their way, they might incite a violent disruption of the march on Monday.

King had heard enough. He fumed: "I'd rather be dead than afraid." He seemed to be blurting out a maxim to steady his nerves, even if it did not seem to fit the moment. His frustration with the Invaders was spilling over. One of King's aides asked him what he thought about inviting three or four Invaders to join the SCLC staff and paying them a modest salary. The theory was that, as staff members under King's sway, the Invaders would adhere to a philosophy of nonviolence.[11]

Hosea Williams pressed the point. On questions of tactics, along with James Bevel, Williams occupied the hawkish end of the spectrum among the SCLC executive staff. It was Williams who persuaded King to approve a march across the Edmund Pettus Bridge at Selma into a phalanx of Alabama state troopers. It was a highly daring plan that risked ending in a bloodbath for the marchers, which is exactly what happened.

As the meeting dragged on, Williams persisted in arguing that the Invaders' notion of tactical violence had merit. King would have none of it. He rejected any hedging on the bedrock principle of nonviolence. As historian Adam Fairclough would write: "Refusing to let the matter drop, King paced the room, preaching to his staff."[12] King was not usually a pacer. In Memphis he could not resist pacing.

On this afternoon King might well have questioned his strategy for rechanneling Black Power anger into nonviolent protest. The strategy rested on a basic idea: that he could succeed in persuading Black Power groups like the Invaders to fall into line behind his style of protest. With the Poor People's Campaign only weeks away, the objective seemed all the more critical.

Yet the radical tilt of SNCC under H. Rap Brown's leadership was threatening to King's agenda, and Brown's inflammatory rhetoric could hardly have been reassuring to King. A speech to an already angered crowd in Cambridge, Maryland, in 1967 had resulted in Brown's arrest for inciting the riot that followed.[13] The arrest did not delegitimize him among masses of angry inner-city youths. On the contrary: for many, the rage he was expressing was theirs.

As he sought broad support for the Poor People's Campaign, King had witnessed Brown's aggressive tactics firsthand. In February 1968, Brown had barged into an SCLC board meeting in a Washington church. He had brought along walkie-talkie-carrying toughs as bodyguards. They had disrupted the meeting, even barring some of the board members from entering the room.[14]

King nonetheless continued to believe that he could redirect even the angry extremism of Brown's followers into nonviolent protest to confront the government in Washington. He would convince Black Power militants that his nonviolent movement to end poverty was not meek or passive but a militant civil disobedience. In his history of the SCLC, Fairclough explains King's strategy this way: "Young blacks could be won to nonviolence, King believed, if they had a chance to join a movement of sufficient militancy and power."[15]

Now in Memphis King was assuming that, if he could draw the Invaders into the movement on his terms, they would come to recognize nonviolent protest as a great force for social change. They would recognize his leadership to advance a common purpose. Their cooperation, he imagined, would be the linchpin to keeping the march on April 6 peaceful.

It was a dubious assumption. It was not the Invaders who had broken windows and looted stores on March 28 in Memphis. Few of them were in the marchers' ranks, according to an FBI after-action report.[16] Rather, as James Lawson would say, the rioters were "small time shoplifters and thieves in the Beale Street area who took advantage of the march to loot stores."[17]

There was little evidence that the Invaders caused the riot, and they were denying that they had. But they meant for King to believe that they could prevent a riot from happening again. If he believed that, they had bargaining power. An FBI informant close to the Invaders reported: "Cabbage and his group want to give the illusion that they are the only force which can control militant Negro youths in Memphis and can prevent trouble."[18]

It did appear that the Invaders had something of a following in the city's high schools. Some students were intrigued enough by the group's rhetoric to outfit themselves in jackets emblazoned with the word "Invaders" across the back. The youths wore the jackets "as a symbol of self-identity with Black Power," not necessarily because they were allied with the Invaders or would follow their instructions, the FBI informant said.[19]

If King succeeded in recruiting the Invaders to his cause, he expected them to mobilize a significant number of parade marshals. Cabbage was promising twenty-five. But how many could he deliver? His core group totaled only ten to fifteen adherents. It was a loose-knit bunch. There was no membership roll. There were no dues. They had no resources to speak of. They had conferred on Marrell McCollough, the undercover policeman posing as an Invader, the lofty title of minister of transportation. He earned the title because he owned a car.[20] "Largely ineffective" was how Robert Blakey, the counsel of a congressional committee that would investigate the Invaders, summed up the militants' sway over the "younger, more disillusioned" blacks in Memphis.[21]

By Thursday afternoon, King no longer had any illusions about the Black Power group. He had come to see them as a distraction and a menace. As the staff meeting wound down, King said there was no point in continuing to negotiate. Hosea Williams conceded the point. He left the meeting to look for Charles Cabbage. When he found Cabbage, he delivered a blunt message: the SCLC did not regard the Invaders as trustworthy, and their refusal to renounce violence made them unfit to take part in the march on Monday.[22] Williams ordered the Invaders to vacate their motel rooms for arriving guests to occupy.

At 5:50 p.m. all the Invaders spilled out of Room 315, toting bags, and quickly left the Lorraine. They left without paying their room and food costs totaling $167. The SCLC was stuck with the tab.[23]

In their rush to Memphis neither King nor his staff had had enough time to learn much about the city's inner workings. King, lacking an understanding of the racial politics of Memphis, had misjudged the Invaders.

Chapter 19

Melancholy Afternoon

*I can't take it anymore. I'm going to the country
to stay with one of my members. I need to go
to the farm, and I'm going down there.*

—MLK, comment to Ralph Abernathy, as he
contemplated returning to Memphis,
March 30, 1968

THE SURVEILLANCE DETAIL of officers Ed Redditt and Willie Richmond was on the King watch for a second day. They were still entrenched in their observation post in the back of Fire Station #2 across Mulberry Street from the Lorraine Motel. They had observed members of the Invaders and the SCLC staff buzzing from room to room of the motel as they gathered for meetings.[1] They would report no sightings of King all morning or afternoon.

King remained in Room 306 for much of the morning, leaving only to confront Dorothy Cotton and eat lunch in the motel dining room. Once he and Abernathy had finished their catfish, they returned to the room. They were hoping for word from Andrew Young about the outcome of the hearing in Judge Brown's courtroom.

They had heard nothing from Young all morning. They feared that a prolonged hearing meant bad news, that the judge would not vacate the injunction.[2] If Young had called, he could have informed them that the testimony by three Memphis police officials had lasted all morning and that Young and Lawson were to testify after a lunch break.

While waiting for word from the courthouse, King busied himself on the phone. He telephoned SCLC headquarters in Atlanta, asking his secretary, Dora McDonald, for messages. He called Harry Wachtel, a back-channel lawyer and confidante of King, at his New York law firm.[3] He called Ebenezer to notify church officials about the theme and title of his Sunday sermon. It would reflect his somber mood at the time. The title was: "Why America May Go to Hell." King had found time to plan the sermon even as he grappled with the crisis in Memphis. He was able to convey a point-by-point preview to McDonald.[4]

With still no word from Young, King went downstairs to Georgia Davis's Room 201. His brother, A.D., was already in the room, along with Lukey Ward and Davis. It did not surprise Davis that King preferred her room to his. King was well aware that the FBI had been bugging his hotel rooms, among other places. He was constantly suspicious of possible FBI eavesdropping.[5] To prevent government monitoring of their conversation, he and Coretta sometimes even went so far as to talk in code.[6]

Not that King and A.D. discussed anything all that sensitive while they were in Room 201. Giddy to be together again and seized by an adolescent impulse, the brothers telephoned their mother in Atlanta. They talked to her for almost an hour. Indulging an urge for boyish mischief, they teased her. Alberta, whom everyone called Mama King, did not seem like a mother who would have had much tolerance for her sons' foolishness. A short, stocky woman who dressed meticulously, an accomplished church organist, she had an air of formality about her. She did not call her husband, Martin Sr., by his first name. To her he was always Reverend King.[7] But according to Coretta, her dignified mother-in-law actually had a "keen sense of humor."[8]

Taking turns on the phone, King and A.D. pretended to be the other. That kept their mother guessing which was which. The more they confounded her, the more they laughed. Whoops and hoots filled the room. Turning serious, Mrs. King expressed her distress about the rioting in Memphis the week before. She handed the phone to Daddy King.[9] He expressed his concern as well. To relieve his parents of worry, King said that everything was fine in Memphis. Back on the phone, Alberta gushed about how happy she was that her sons were together.

The warmth and cheer from his parents buoyed King. Once he was off the phone, however, his mood darkened. He seemed pensive, distracted.

King remained flat on his back in bed for much of the afternoon, awake, saying little, staring blankly at the ceiling, lost in his thoughts. "Most of the day, he was just resting and relaxing," Davis would recall.[10]

He had much to mull over, moments fresh on his mind. The bomb threat to his plane from Atlanta, the outpouring of mournful emotions in his speech at Mason Temple, Dorothy Cotton's angry departure from the Lorraine, the futility of his attempt to enlist the Invaders as parade marshals—they were all unsettling events in his life since the morning before.

As he struggled with the Memphis crisis, he was still hearing a drumbeat of criticism against him for his stand against the Vietnam War. Top union leaders were continuing to object, as were some prominent civil rights leaders.[11] Among the union leaders continuing to take issue with him over Vietnam were longtime friends and allies such as Roy Wilkins and Whitney Young. The criticism grated on him. Close friend Marian Logan would tell of his acute anguish because of his friends' disagreement with him over Vietnam. She would recall: "I don't think it was because he doubted the position he had taken, that it was wrong. I think he felt badly that a lot of people didn't agree with him or couldn't understand his reason for taking a stand. It depressed him terribly."[12]

He could hardly have been happy, moreover, about being trapped another day in the city where rioting had so subverted his reputation. Critics from all sides were questioning his relevance as a nonviolent leader. Even he was losing hope. In the article for the issue of *Look* magazine slated for April 16, 1968, he wrote: "As committed as I am to nonviolence, I have to face this fact: If we do not get a positive response in Washington, many more Negroes will begin to think and act in violent terms."[13]

Very likely nothing troubled King more, as he stared at the ceiling of Room 201, than the fading prospects of the Poor People's Campaign. As a consequence of the rioting in Memphis, he was stranded in a motel room rather than on the move to recruit and organize for the antipoverty drive set to begin in just eighteen days.

Even before the crisis in Memphis, the mobilization of King's army of poor people was lagging. Then, with five weeks to go before the scheduled kickoff of the Washington campaign, Hosea Williams was lamenting the slow pace of recruitment. In a memo to SCLC staff, Williams, the campaign's field director, wrote: "Yes, many meetings are being held, some money is being raised, but hardly anyone is being recruited for the long, hard drive in Washington." Williams added that he was "very much disturbed" by the lack of progress.[14]

Money was being raised, but it was far from enough to meet the heavy costs they expected to incur in Washington. At the SCLC money had always been tight. In 1965, when its staff roster totaled 150 people, the budget was shy of a million dollars.[15] To cover its expenses, the SCLC relied on the uneven flow of direct-mail appeals and King's income as a writer and speaker. At times only emergency bailouts from labor unions or fund-raising performances by celebrities such as Harry Belafonte and Aretha Franklin kept the SCLC afloat.[16]

King was counting on the pastors of African American churches to promote the Washington campaign. Some were proving to be less supportive than he had expected. As the FBI would note in field reports, a group of 150 pastors King had convened in Miami to enlist as boosters in the antipoverty drive "had remained noncommittal" despite his impassioned plea for help.[17]

Even some of King's long-devoted benefactors were abandoning him. Labor union dollars were barely trickling in, and King seemed at a loss what to do about it.[18] The reasons varied: a shift of liberals' attention from civil rights to Vietnam, a backlash against inner-city rioting, and doubts about the Poor People's Campaign.[19] So little money was coming in during February that William Rutherford, the executive director of the SCLC, wrote an urgent plea to Marlon Brando. Rutherford said that the SCLC's needs were great, and he appealed to the celebrated actor to sponsor a "fundraising soiree" in Hollywood to support the antipoverty campaign.[20] Years later, reflecting on the state of the SCLC's finances in the spring of 1968, Ralph Abernathy would say, "We were getting ready to launch the largest campaign that ever had taken place within this country, the Poor People's Campaign, and we just didn't have the money."[21]

The SCLC treasury had been far short of the needed sums in late February when King agreed to speak at a rally in Memphis for the striking garbage workers. The timing suggested that he might have scheduled the speech to prop up the SCLC's finances as it embarked on the Poor People's Campaign. Dramatizing the impoverished plight of the garbage workers could have inspired support for the campaign in the form of money and volunteers.

The budgetary picture brightened somewhat the next month. A fervent direct mail letter signed by King yielded a $15,000 cascade of checks in a single day.[22] Volunteers were signing on in numbers that promised to exceed the minimum target of two hundred persons per city or state in some locations.[23]

But by the end of March, as the FBI recorded in a wiretap, Rutherford was warning about an alarming shortfall between receipts and the extraordinary expense to transport, feed, and shelter three thousand volunteers for weeks, perhaps months.[24] What's more, according to Rutherford, King was so concerned about the lack of progress in recruiting volunteers that he was reassigning Hosea Williams, Bernard Lafayette, James Bevel, and Andrew Young to devote themselves to that priority.

As King brooded about the deficit of money and volunteers, another question was nagging at him. How would the American public respond to the massive civil disobedience that he was planning? He knew it would not be easy to build the groundswell of public support that would cause Washington lawmakers to approve the multibillion-dollar antipoverty programs he was demanding. He would succeed only if he could win broad popular support for his sweeping plan to end poverty. At a retreat for SCLC staff at Ebenezer Church on King's thirty-ninth birthday, January 15, 1968, he conceded that taxpayers might recoil against his plan. He said, "It's really going to cost billions of dollars, and, as a result of that, many people find themselves resisting."[25]

King knew too that powerful forces were already converging to oppose the Poor People's Campaign. Out of public view President Johnson was demanding that King call the whole thing off. Publicly, referring obliquely to the expected protests in Washington, Johnson vowed that he would oppose lawlessness "in whatever form and in whatever guise."[26]

In the article for *Look* magazine King acknowledged the roadblock that his legislative agenda would encounter in Congress. Calling it a "coalition-dominated, rural-dominated, basically Southern Congress," he wrote, "There are Southerners there with committee chairmanships, and they are going to stand in the way of progress as long as they can."[27] The US Supreme Court, which had vindicated the movement's right to free speech and assembly in a string of First Amendment cases, seemed to be tilting the other way. In *Walker v. Birmingham*, the high court upheld, on June 5, 1967, King's conviction for violating an Alabama judge's injunction barring him from leading a march.

Not known to King were the dirty tricks being readied by J. Edgar Hoover to thwart the Poor People's Campaign. Hoover was intensifying the smear campaign against King that had been ongoing for years. He was ordering FBI agents around the country to cook up various schemes. One would falsely link King to the highly controversial Nation of Islam in order to derail fund-raising. Another would spread disinformation to muddle King's speaking schedule and frustrate prospective volunteers. Yet a third would falsely warn that participants in the antipoverty mobilization would lose their welfare checks. A special agent pretending to be a businessman already had called the SCLC office in Detroit offering buses to transport volunteers to Washington. The FBI had no intention of providing buses. It was a ruse that would dishearten volunteers and might deter them from going to Washington altogether.[28]

Despite the melancholy that seemed to engulf King that Thursday afternoon, he emerged from his lethargy for brief spells of conversation and laughter. He turned chatty when lawyer Chauncey Eskridge and an SCLC aide stopped by. But King did not leave the room. He did not join his friend Billy Kyles and aide Jesse Jackson elsewhere at the Lorraine to sing along with bandleader Ben Branch. The band, an arm of Operation Breadbasket, had flown in from Chicago to play at the pro-strike rally scheduled for that night at Mason Temple. At the Lorraine the band was rehearsing gospel hymns. One of them was entitled "I'm So Glad Trouble Don't Always Last," which seemed aptly chosen as a tonic for the troubles in Memphis."[29]

Abernathy, who had returned to Room 306 for a nap, rejoined King downstairs at about four o'clock. Not long after, Andrew Young knocked at the door. Davis opened, and Young bounded in. Davis would recount what happened next.

Young turned to King. "The judge says you better not march," Young said. "They gonna lock you up if you march."

Everyone laughed, except King. He said, tersely, "We'll go on and march regardless of what they say." He did not seem amused.

"Nah," Young said. "We can march as long as it's peaceful."

In a flash King grabbed a pillow and pitched it at Young, who lobbed it back to him. Peals of laughter filled the room.

Young briefed King on the day's events in court. A march, Lucius Burch had told Judge Brown, was certain to occur with or without King at the head of it. In crafty cross-examination, Burch had then maneuvered Police Director Holloman into conceding a central point. Holloman had admitted that he would prefer a march under King's leadership committed to nonviolence than a march that proceeded without him. That line of argument had carried the day. Brown had said he would allow King to march provided he agreed to certain safeguards: there must be enough trained marshals on hand, and the organizers of the march must coordinate their plans with the police. Lawson and Young had assured the judge that King would abide by those terms.

It was about 5:30 when King told the people gathered in Room 201 of the Lorraine, "I want to go upstairs and freshen up." He wanted time to dress before he left for dinner. King and the whole SCLC staff in Memphis were invited to the house of Billy Kyles and his wife, Gwen, for soul food. The dinner would precede the night's rally at Mason Temple.

Back in their room, King and Abernathy had visions of soul food dancing in their heads. They knew Gwen Kyles to be an excellent cook. Imagining what food she might serve that night had King and Abernathy salivating. King said to Abernathy, "Ralph, call her up and ask her what she's having."[30]

"You're not kidding, are you?" Abernathy replied.

"No," King said. "Call her."

Abernathy called Mrs. Kyles. She ticked off the menu: roast beef, asparagus, cauliflower, candied yams, pigs' feet, and chitlins. Delighted by the menu, King went into the bathroom to shave. In King's case shaving was a particularly onerous chore. In deference to his tender skin, he shaved not with a razor but a depilatory powder called "Magic Shave." He had to plaster it on and wait for it to erode the hair.

While King was waiting for the laborious shaving procedure to run its course, Abernathy mentioned a scheduling conflict. On days Abernathy was scheduled to be in Washington, he had to preach at the weeklong revival of the West Hunter Street Baptist Church in Atlanta. Turning to Abernathy, King said, "Ralph, I would never think of going to Washington without you. West Hunter is the best church in the world. They'll do anything for you. You go tell them you're going to have a different kind of revival, one in which we are going to review the soul of this nation. Will you do it?" Sighing, Abernathy promised.

Billy Kyles knocked on the door to tell King that dinner was at six and to please hurry along. It was 5:55 p.m. King splashed some cologne on his face. He told Abernathy, "I'll wait on the balcony," and he exited the room.

Chapter 20

Ray's Lucky Breaks

This is what is going to happen to me also.

—MLK, reacting to the assassination
of President Kennedy, November 22, 1963

JAMES EARL RAY likely slept in on the morning of April 4. He did not check out of the New Rebel until early that Thursday afternoon. As was his habit, he bought a copy of the local paper—in the case of Memphis, that was the morning daily, the *Commercial Appeal.* He must have zeroed in quickly on a front-page story headlined "King Challenges Court Restraint, Vows to March."

The story said that King was back in Memphis preparing for the march on Monday. It explained, though, that Judge Brown's injunction might block him from leading the march. The story quoted King's comment the day before that he might disregard such an injunction "on the basis of conscience."

One detail buried in the tenth paragraph would have had Ray riveted to the story. He was on a mission to kill King, and he knew how he would do it. He would shoot him. Where he could find King was another question. If he had not learned where King was staying from the TV news the night before, the newspaper would have clued him in. It identified the Lorraine Motel as King's lodging while he was in Memphis.

Determining King's likely whereabouts so quickly and effortlessly from a TV broadcast or a ten-cent newspaper was the first of several lucky breaks that would advantage Ray's murderous plan.

In the early afternoon, he left the New Rebel in his Mustang heading to the Lorraine. From the New Rebel it is a ten-mile drive through the city's southwestern flank to the motel. Very likely Ray cruised the area around the Lorraine, scouting for a covert location from which he might observe King's movements. Roaming the seedy area around the motel would have pointed him to four red brick buildings, none taller than four stories, which formed the 400 block of South Main. The Lorraine faced the rear of the four buildings across Mulberry Street.

Ray likely cased the 400 block of South Main, hoping that from inside one of the four buildings he might find a window that would afford him an unobstructed view of the motel. On the same logic, police officers Redditt and Richmond had picked the back of the fire station at 474 South Main as their surveillance post from where they could monitor King and his associates. Unlike Redditt and Richmond, Ray would not only have to locate the right building. He would also have to be fortunate enough to find a way to enter and remain in it long enough to get a bead on King.

Luck was on Ray's side again. He was able to find just the place that suited his purpose. It was the rooming house at 418½–422½ South Main: two adjoining brick buildings, each two stories tall. On the ground floor were two businesses, Jim's Grill and Canipe Amusement Company, a jukebox repair and record shop. To the left of the Canipe storefront, an entrance opened to a stairway leading to the rooming-house office on the second floor.

It was about 3:15 p.m. when Ray parked the Mustang nine blocks away, probably to distance the car far from the rooming house so no one could link it to his having been on the 400 block of South Main. He walked to the entrance of the rooming house, climbed the stairs, and knocked at the door of the office.

Bessie Brewer, the resident manager, interrupted her bookkeeping to answer the door. An ample woman in her thirties, she was wearing faded blue jeans and a checkered shirt, and her hair was in rollers. Her sixteen-unit establishment catered to hard-up transients. Ray, who was no stranger to derelict rooming houses, would belittle it later as a "wino place."[1] Its residents were not far removed from homelessness, and Brewer had learned to exercise caution. When Ray knocked, she opened the door a crack, leaving its chain latch closed, and gazed at Ray.

"Do you have a room to rent?" he asked through the door, as Brewer would relate to author Gerold Frank.[2] In Frank's account, she would remember Ray as a "trim white man who appeared to be in his early thirties," having "dark hair, blue eyes, and a thin nose" and wearing "a dark suit that seemed much too nice for the neighborhood." Reassured, she opened the door to admit him. "He was a clean, neat man," she would tell a reporter for the *Commercial Appeal* a day later.

Brewer motioned to Ray to follow her across from the office to the first door on the left. It was Room 8, a kitchenette apartment that rented for $10.50 a week. It had a stove and refrigerator. Ray glanced around. The room was not on the side of the building facing Mulberry Street. "I only want a sleeping room," he told Brewer.

She led him through a second-floor passageway to Room 5B in the adjoining building. To enter Room 5B, Brewer had to open a padlock on the door and turn a jury-rigged doorknob fashioned from a coat hanger. The rent was less, $8.50 a week, she told Ray. The room looked as humble as the door lock. A naked lightbulb dangled from the ceiling. A mattress on a metal bed frame sagged. There was a worn wooden dresser and a single window behind tattered, floral-patterned curtains. Ray glanced inside and said the room was fine. He would take it.

During its investigation a decade later, the House Select Committee on Assassinations would find no evidence that Ray had checked out the view from the window before taking Room 5B. Rather, the committee concluded, "the privacy and its location at the rear of the building apparently made the room more acceptable to Ray" than Room 8.[3]

Back in Brewer's office, she asked him to pay for the room in advance. He dipped into his pocket for a crisp $20 bill and handed it to her. As she wrote a receipt, she asked his name. He said it was John Willard. To Brewer he seemed pleasant and calm. He even smiled reassuringly. Only after he left the office did something about him strike her as odd. He did not ask for the padlock to lock the door of Room 5B. Nor did he have any luggage.

A half hour later, Ray turned up at the York Arms Company, a sporting goods store on South Main four blocks north of the Lorraine. Ray asked a store clerk, Ralph Carpenter, to show him a pair of binoculars. Carpenter would comment later on his impression of Ray and how he was struck by the quaint neatness of the slender man. Ray's dark hair was combed straight back, and he wore a narrow, old-fashioned knit tie.

The clerk offered two of the store's pricier models, one pair of binoculars for $200 and another for $90. Ray asked for something cheaper. He was shown a pair of 7x35 Bushnell Banner binoculars. The price was $40, plus $1.55 tax. Ray nodded his approval. He dug into his pocket and slowly counted out two twenties, a one-dollar bill, two quarters, and, finally, five pennies.[4]

Equipped with the binoculars, Ray drove back to the rooming house. This time he parked a few doors south, at 424 South Main. He sat in the car for a few moments, scarcely moving, seemingly staring into space. Or so it appeared to Elizabeth Copeland and Frances Thompson, two employees at the Seabrook Wallpaper store across the street. They observed him frozen to the driver's seat and wondered about this.[5] He may have remained in the car until he believed nobody was around and he could exit the car unseen.

When he did exit the Mustang, he opened the trunk and removed a bulging bundle wrapped in a green and brown bedspread. The bedspread most likely cloaked the Remington Gamemaster rifle that Ray had bought in Birmingham, a portable transistor radio etched with his inmate number (00416) from the Missouri State Penitentiary, a pair of men's undershorts, an undershirt, a hairbrush, various tools and toiletries, and at least two cans of Schlitz beer.[6] He wrapped the bundle in his arms and managed at the same time to grip in one hand the York Arms bag containing his new field glasses. He hastened the few steps to the rooming house entrance and climbed the twenty stairs to Room 5B.

It was not long after 5:00 p.m. when he entered the room. Outside it was cool, and the sky was clear. The sun would not set till six twenty-five. As it would turn out, luck was again on his side. He could count on plenty of light for almost an hour and a half.

In his room, Ray hooked the curtain out of the way, raised the window, removed the screen, and canvassed the area. Room 5B was located near the rear of the building on the east side, which stood at a ninety-degree angle from Mulberry Street. By leaning out the window and craning his neck to the left, he could look diagonally across Mulberry. From that angle the Lorraine came into full view. His good luck was holding. Room 5B afforded him a view of the motel.

Yet as a lookout it was not ideal. To see the whole expanse of the Lorraine, Ray had to lean out the window. He would have to expose his head outside as he surveyed the area with binoculars. A vigilant passerby on South Main might have been struck by a man's head jutting out the window, with binoculars trained toward the Lorraine. A police security detail protecting King at the Lorraine, if there had been one, might have seen the man with the binoculars, been suspicious, and investigated.

Six rooms on the same floor as Ray's shared a dingy bathroom at the end of a linoleum hallway. The faded green walls were smudged and peeling. The only light was a bulb screwed into a ceiling socket. There was a toilet, a small sink below a pitted mirror, and, off to the left underneath the single window, a bathtub. From Room 5B it was ten steps down the hallway.

The occupants of Room 6B, next to Ray's, were Charles Stephens and his bedridden, common-law wife, Grace.[7] Stephens was forty-six, a heavy equipment operator who had been forced by tuberculosis to retire when he was not yet thirty. He would tell investigators that in the late afternoon he heard the scraping of furniture being moved across the floor of the new lodger's room. It was the sound of Ray pushing the chest of drawers away from the lone window. He might have heard Ray moving a straight-backed wooden chair and positioning it close to the window.

When Ray sat in the chair and leaned far out the window, the Lorraine came fully into view. But from that vantage point the motel lay at an angle that would complicate firing a bullet in that direction. Still, it afforded him an adequate perch for watching the Lorraine.

As his new neighbor stirred, Stephens continued to listen through the thin walls. He heard footsteps as Ray strode to the end of the hall and entered the bathroom. Stephens would recall that the man entered the bathroom twice, each time staying only a few minutes. One time Ray flushed the toilet. He returned to the bathroom yet a third time, staying what seemed like a long time to Stephens. He listened impatiently for the man to leave because he was anxious to use the toilet. He was not alone. Willie Anschutz, who occupied Room 4B, also needed the toilet. Anschutz knocked on the bathroom door, which was latched. No response.

Before Ray entered the bathroom, he likely had been peering from the window of Room 5B, his eyes glued on the Lorraine. It is probable that he saw King leave Room 201 at about 5:30 and climb the exterior stairway of the motel to the second floor before entering his room. It was another lucky break. The timing coincided with Stephens's estimate of when Ray padded to the bathroom the third time.[8]

Fortunate to have the bathroom available at that moment, Ray latched the door and prepared a sniper's nest. Off to one side next to the only window stood a claw-foot bathtub. It was small and antique, with sides that were rust-stained and chipped. Ray climbed into the tub and crouched next to the window. He must have been elated when he looked out the window. He had an excellent view of the Lorraine. The whole of the motel came into clear focus two hundred and seven feet away.

Ray yanked the window open and shoved its mesh screen outward. The screen clattered into the backyard. Through the binoculars the Lorraine appeared to be thirty feet away. The Redfield scope mounted on his Remington Gamemaster had the same magnification. He unsheathed the rifle from its blue, zippered carrying case and flipped open the box of soft-point ammunition.[9]

The army had taught Ray to fire a rifle with a degree of accuracy. He knew enough to pose the Gamemaster firmly on the window ledge. He pressed the muzzle down hard enough to dent the ledge slightly. And he waited.

Chapter 21

Dark Night

In a sense our nation is climbing a mountain . . .
and now we are in the most difficult
and trying stages.

—MLK, talk at Waycross, Georgia, March 22, 1968

IT WAS A FEW MINUTES before 6:00 p.m. on Thursday, April 4. The temperature in Memphis was in the mid-fifties, down from the seventies that morning. Despite the chill, King was not warmly dressed as he exited Room 306. He was wearing his customary dark suit, a conservative yellow and black tie, white shirt, and black shoes.

Freshly shaved, with cologne refreshing his face, he was primed for the much-anticipated dinner at Billy Kyles's house. To finish shaving and dressing for the occasion, Abernathy stayed behind in their room. He wanted to look his best for the night out. He told King that he would be along directly.

King walked the few steps from Room 306 to the adjacent second-story balcony and paused to wait. He had a commanding view of the Lorraine parking lot below. His aides—Young, Bevel, Williams, Lee, Jackson, and Orange—had gathered in the parking lot. They would be going with him to the Kyles's party. Kyles was waiting for King on the balcony. "People started waving at him," Kyles would recall. "Hey," King hollered, waving back. "Hey. Hey."

In the brisk air, Young and Orange were frolicking about, shadowboxing like kids in a schoolyard. The massive Orange, six foot four and nearly three hundred pounds, towered over Young. Orange's roughneck appearance was deceiving. He was a gentle, nonviolent guy ("sweet" was Young's word for him), but the world did not know that. The sight of his imposing heft added a measure of security on the road for King and his entourage. "Nobody would try to be physical with us with James around," Young would say.[1]

Bemused by the sight of the two men engaged in mock fighting, King bellowed to Young: "Don't hurt him, Andy!"

King spotted Jesse Jackson standing in the parking lot. There had been tension between the two men since their exchange of acid words at the staff meeting in Atlanta on Saturday. In a fence-mending gesture King called down to Jackson: "Jesse, I want you to come to dinner with me."[2]

"Jesse already took care of that," Kyles said, as he started down the stairs from the balcony.

Not to let the matter drop quickly, King shouted: "Jesse, we're going to Billy Kyles's, and you don't even have a tie on."[3] Jackson was dressed in the ruggedly mod style of the sixties: olive turtleneck sweater and unzipped brown leather jacket.

"The prerequisite to eating is an appetite, not a tie," Jackson said.

King laughed. "You're crazy," he said, and everyone laughed with him.

Standing next to Jackson was Ben Branch, the director of the Operation Breadbasket band. Jackson shouted, "Doc, this is Ben Branch. Ben used to live in Memphis. He plays in our band."[4]

"Oh, yes, he's my man," King replied. "How are you, Ben?" Branch, who was a trumpeter as well as bandleader, shouted hello back to King.

"Ben," King said, "I want you to play 'Precious Lord' for me tonight." It was one of King's favorite gospel songs. He would have been aware of its origins as a melancholy lyric written in 1932 by Thomas Dorsey. The full title was "Precious Lord, Take My Hand." It was a plea for God's help to cope with death, and in the case of Dorsey it had been a cry for God's hand to allay the grief he felt over the deaths of his wife and newborn son.

"Sing it real pretty," King said.

"I sure will, Doc," Branch said.

Branch and the others were clustered around a white Cadillac limo. The R. S. Lewis Funeral Home had put the Cadillac and a driver, Solomon Jones, at King's disposal in Memphis.

Jones was waiting in the parking lot for King. Jones cried out, "Dr. King, it's going to be cool tonight. Be sure to carry your coat."

Before King could say a word of thanks, a shot rang out. A bullet struck him on the right side of the face, traveled through his neck, and came to rest on the left side of his back, splintering his spinal column.[5] He collapsed instantly onto the floor of the balcony.

It was 6:01 p.m.

When some of the people closest to King heard the shot, they did not recognize it for what it was. Abernathy was dousing his face with aftershave cologne. He would remember hearing what sounded to him like the backfire of a car. "But there was just enough difference to chill my heart," he would recount years later. When he looked through the open doorway at the balcony adjacent to his room, he saw that King was no longer standing. He was flat on his back, sprawled between the doorway and the balcony's railing.[6]

Andrew Young, who was still horsing around with James Orange in the parking lot, thought he had heard either the backfire of a car or the pop of a firecracker. His eyes turned toward King on the balcony. "I could see where he had fallen down, fallen back," Young would write. "I remember for a moment I thought he was clowning; he had been in such a playful mood."[7]

Billy Kyles was five or six steps down from the balcony, when he heard the report of the rifle. "I thought it was a car backfiring," he would say. Down in the parking lot he saw people suddenly ducking behind cars. Kyles would remember somebody screaming, "Oh, my Lord, they've shot Martin!"[8]

Abernathy bolted through the door of his room to the balcony. He knelt next to King. "Even at the first glance I could see that a bullet had entered his right cheek, leaving a small hole," he would recall. King's eyes seemed to flutter. Abernathy patted his face and said, "Martin, this is Ralph. Can you hear me?" He then saw, as he would put it, "the understanding drain from his eyes and leave them absolutely empty."[9]

Blood was seeping from his wounds, gathering in a pool on the concrete floor beneath his head. By then Young had rushed to the balcony and was leaning over King. Young peered at the blood and the severity of the wounds, how the skin had been ripped from the chin bone. "Oh, God! Ralph. It's over," Abernathy would recall Young saying.[10]

As Abernathy and Young were tending to King, a swarm of police officers, as many as ten of them, were converging on the Lorraine. They were arriving within a minute or two of the time Ray shot King. They were racing to the Lorraine not in patrol cars but on foot.[11] How they arrived so quickly would become a question for investigators. By chance, at 6:01 p.m., the officers had been on a coffee break at Fire Station #2 at South Main and Butler Streets a half block from the Lorraine.

The officers belonged to Police Tactical Unit Ten, one of several created at the outbreak of the garbage workers' strike to respond to emergencies during the crisis. Still at his surveillance post at the back of the fire station and monitoring the Lorraine, Patrolman Willie Richmond had seen, almost immediately, that King was down. Richmond had alerted the officers. They had sprinted to the motel.

It took five minutes or so before a fire department ambulance arrived. King was placed on a stretcher, hustled down the stairs, and lifted into the ambulance.[12]

The ambulance, its siren blaring, raced the two miles north through the heart of downtown Memphis to St. Joseph Hospital. Gregory Jaynes, a young reporter for the *Commercial Appeal*, was hanging out near the police radio monitor in the newsroom when he heard a bulletin that King had been shot. As Jaynes would recount, a copy boy cried, plaintively, "Why here?" A business reporter replied, "Why anywhere?"[13]

The doctors at St. Joseph, recognizing the gravity of King's condition, could do nothing for him. He was pronounced dead at 7:05 p.m. It was forty minutes past sunset. By then the last light in the sky over Memphis had faded to darkness.

In the days before he had returned to the tense city of Memphis, King had been offered his dream job of old. He was invited to take a one-year sabbatical as the interim pastor at the splendid neo-Gothic Riverside Church in New York City.[14] He knew it well. It had a long history serving as a forum for political activism and public debate. From its pulpit King had delivered his passionate speech against the Vietnam War, in 1967. If he had accepted the offer to return to the church in the eminent post as pastor, it would have spared him the travail of returning to Memphis. He had declined the offer.

Four days after King's death at age thirty-nine, Coretta King and Ralph Abernathy led thousands of people on a march through downtown Memphis, mourning King's death and supporting the garbage workers' strike. In her remarks that day, Coretta King spoke of her husband's deepest yearnings, the covenant he had sworn to himself that, by sacrificing himself, dying if necessary, for a cause that was "right and just," his life would end in the most redemptive way possible.[15]

Chapter 22

Redemption

One has to conquer the fear of death if
he is going to do anything constructive in life
and take a stand against evil.

—MLK, comment at news conference
in Los Angeles, February 24, 1965

KING HAD EXPECTED to die a violent death, had accepted the fate as inescapable and reconciled himself to it. But he had not sought martyrdom. A martyr invites death in a quest for glory or heavenly reward. King wanted to live a long life, as he had declared movingly at Mason Temple. He wanted to live, but he had a higher calling. As Ralph Abernathy would say, "He loved life, and he wanted to live, but his commitment to the cause of Christ [and social justice]" was "much more powerful than his personal safety."[1]

By the spring of 1968 King was risking his life in new and hazardous ways, expecting to sacrifice it, willing to pay the ultimate price, in pursuit of his cause. As he saw it, he was risking his life to save the millions of Americans whose lives he believed were being crushed by racial bigotry and poverty.

He had not always been that way. How he came to see his death at an early age as an inevitable and justifiable sacrifice for high moral purpose is a story of his religious soul-searching and sense of grand destiny.

Even Christian theology had not always defined his purpose. As a student at Morehouse College he did not profess a deeply religious faith. He disavowed the bodily resurrection of Jesus. He lost interest in the church as a career. He opted to study not for the ministry but for medicine and then, when that seemed unattainable, law.[2]

By the end of his senior year, though, he had yielded to his father's wishes that he enter the ministry. He enrolled at Crozer Theological Seminary and embarked on a path to become a Baptist pastor and scholar of theology. That was his goal.

In 1955, he accepted the pulpit at the Dexter Avenue Church in Montgomery, Alabama, as his first job after satisfying most of the requirements for his PhD in theology from Boston University. His immediate goal was putting the final touches on his dissertation to complete the degree.

He chose the church in Montgomery with an eye toward improving race relations in at least one harshly segregated city of the Deep South.[3] That was not, however, his primary reason for going to Montgomery. He envisioned the pastor's job at Dexter as a way station. He would serve long enough to gain experience pastoring a church. He would check that box ("ministry to an African American community in a small Southern city") en route to a career as a theologian. He would be an ivory tower scholar, a teacher, and a pastor. "When he first started to preach," Andrew Young would say later, "Martin's ambition was to teach at a top-notch seminary and become the preacher at a place like Riverside Church, the big church on the Upper West Side of Manhattan."[4]

Nor had King always sought the end of poverty as his overriding mission or called for anything on the scale of massive, militant civil disobedience in the nation's capital to force far-reaching political change.

As a college student, he showed little interest in politics. He was said to be bookish or frivolous, depending on who was recollecting his interests at that time. No one remembered him as political. Maxine Smith, who knew him as a sophomore at Morehouse when she was a freshman at nearby Spelman College, remembered him as studious, often lugging a load of books that he "carried under an umbrella."[5] Others recalled his penchant for frivolity, especially dancing and playing cards.[6]

By the time he reached Boston University for doctoral study he was exhibiting a serious political intent. He was intrigued by leftist political theory. In a letter to Coretta, whom he was courting at the time, he wrote that capitalism "has brought about a system that takes necessities from the masses to give luxuries to the classes." He went on, "I would certainly welcome the day to come when there would be nationalization of industry."[7]

If King's misgivings about capitalism stayed with him beyond his student days, he kept his views to himself. He knew that his leftist notions would offend many Americans. He avoided sharp anticapitalist rhetoric, and he went to great pains to disassociate himself from communism. In his first book, *Stride Toward Freedom*, published in 1958, he leveled only a veiled critique of capitalism as inducing people to be "more concerned about making a living than making a life."[8] Communism he rejected flatly for what he regarded as its materialistic view of history, ethical relativism, and political totalitarianism.[9]

His affinity for leftist politics coincided with his interest in a theological doctrine known as the social gospel. The term *social gospel* crystallized a body of thought that had emerged in American theological circles during the first half of the twentieth century. The idea was to bring Christian ethics to bear on social problems, such as racial and economic injustice. When he was barely in his twenties, studying at Crozer, King embraced the social gospel as the core of his theology.[10]

As it turned out, his move to Montgomery allowed him to put the concept of social gospel into practice to an extent that must have surpassed his greatest expectations. That story is well known. He found himself in a hotbed of racial oppression that ignited the city's bus boycott and propelled him to civil rights leadership and national prominence. It had happened almost against his will. As he admitted in 1956, "If anybody had asked me a year ago to lead this movement, I tell you very honestly, I would have run a mile to get away from it."[11]

In Montgomery he discovered the high price that he would have to pay as a nationally prominent leader of the movement. His family then comprised a wife and baby daughter, Yolanda, whom he and Coretta called Yoki. The phone rang incessantly at the house. Callers screamed threats. The family's life seemed in constant danger.

As King recognized what a high price he was paying for his political activism, a profound distress gripped him. On a sleepless night in late January 1956, a tortured King struggled to come to terms with the horror of it all. As he would write in *Stride Toward Freedom*, he bowed his head over the kitchen table and prayed aloud. Whereupon, he heard an inner voice saying to him: "Stand up for righteousness, stand up for truth, and God will be at your side forever." The reservoir of strength and faith he found within himself that night, he would write, prepared him to face anything.[12]

As the movement pushed him more deeply toward the life of a national civil rights figure and he rose to the challenge, he redefined himself. His self-image acquired a new, larger dimension. Fate seemed to be calling him to a higher purpose. "This is not the life I expected to lead," he told Coretta in 1958 after being released from jail in Montgomery. But events had swept him along, and gradually he came to view the movement as his calling and had given himself utterly to it.[13]

Giving himself utterly to the movement meant accepting the risk that he might die a violent death at any moment. He found comfort in the Christian concept that noble sacrifice for others had a "redemptive" value. Christian theology had adapted the word *redemption* from its usage in the Old Testament. In the earlier version, *redemption* had a specific meaning: paying a ransom to free or redeem a slave from bondage. In Christian theology the concept of redemption referred to the death of Jesus, a sacrifice to atone for the sins of others so that they might achieve eternal salvation.

By 1960 King was saying, in effect, that he had embedded the concept into his own psychic fiber. That year he published an essay in a Christian magazine explaining why he had reconciled himself to suffering in the struggle for freedom. "Recognizing the necessity for suffering," he wrote, "I have tried to make it a virtue"—as a means to "heal" people afflicted by racism. The suffering he could justify by living "with the conviction that unearned suffering is redemptive."[14] That is, the sacrifice of his life would have redemptive value if he died in a virtuous quest for social injustice

Had he been less deeply religious or courageous, he might have been less outspoken, lowered his public profile, and minimized the risk of violent death. Instead, he doubled down. Within a few years, he was demanding not just racial desegregation and voting rights but total relief from poverty as a citizen's fundamental right. He couched the idea in the name of redemption of a different kind.

The idea cropped up in his "I Have a Dream" address at the Washington Mall on August 28, 1963. He lamented that African Americans were living on "a lonely island of poverty," and he portrayed the Declaration of Independence as a "promissory note" that the federal government must redeem. If all Americans had a God-given right to life, liberty, and the pursuit of happiness, King reasoned, that promise translated into the government's obligation to alleviate poverty.

In the glow of the "I Have a Dream" speech, he was ever more visible on the national stage. He was awarded the Nobel Peace Prize, and in his acceptance speech at Oslo he said grandly, "I accept this prize for all men who love peace and brotherhood."[15] *Time* magazine put him on its cover. He had a private audience with Pope Paul VI. He met in the Oval Office with Presidents Kennedy and Johnson. By and by, he had come to see himself in a more exalted light. As journalist David Halberstam would say, he had "finally come to believe his myth."[16]

His scope of purpose widened in proportion to his self-image. He dedicated himself to pursuit of a mammoth federal program to end poverty, once and for all. In 1964 he called on Congress to pass a Bill of Rights for the Disadvantaged. It called on the government to devote, in his words, the "full resources of the society . . . to attack the tenacious poverty which so paradoxically exists in the midst of plenty."[17]

When Congress did not respond as he hoped, he determined that he would bring greater political force to bear, and it needed to happen urgently. His answer was the Poor People's Campaign. He imagined that his intervening in the garbage workers' strike would further that mission. So he had gone to Memphis.

In the *Look* article published in the early spring of 1968, he explained why he was making poverty his paramount concern. He wrote, "If something isn't done to deal with the very harsh and real economic problems of the ghetto, the talk of guerrilla warfare [among black militants] is going to become much more real." Further, he expressed alarm that a continuing surge of riots in the nation's inner cities might "strengthen the right wing of the country, and we'll end up with a kind of right-wing take-over and a fascist development" that would be "terribly injurious to the nation."[18]

If King was right in saying that a massive federal antipoverty program would spare the country the calamity of widespread rioting and fascism, it followed that it was a matter of the greatest urgency. But he was not optimistic that the public would rally quickly behind his costly proposal to end poverty. He expected stiff political resistance to a program that would vastly redistribute wealth and power.

His was a far-reaching ideology—"revolutionary," he called it. His vision of the federal government providing a minimal income or guaranteed job for all Americans would have fit neatly into the platform of a European socialist. For the Poor People's Campaign to succeed, Washington lawmakers had to agree to adopt a system of that kind—a system at odds with the American tradition of free enterprise and limited government. How likely was that to happen?

Even Michael Harrington, the socialist activist and astute writer, had his doubts that King would prevail in Washington. Harrington said that bringing thousands of poor people to lay siege to the government in the name of antipoverty relief could "make a strong moral point," but he did not think it would "register as a victory in the public eye."[19]

King himself doubted he would see the response he desired from Congress and the president. As he confided in Young, he expected the powers that be to come down heavily on him in Washington. He expected that his civil disobedience would land him in jail yet again. He might be there a long time.

Young would remember telling him, "If we get locked up in jail, it's not going to be any thirty or sixty days. You're going to get three to five years."

King replied, "That would be just the right amount of time. We would be strong enough, spiritually, coming out of jail to really transform this nation."[20]

Perhaps he knew of the government's delayed response to the kind of grievance that had triggered the veterans' Bonus March in Washington in 1932. Though President Hoover had not supported their demand for a bonus and had forcibly removed the veterans from their makeshift camp, their protest may not have been entirely in vain. It may have led Congress to enact educational benefits for World War II veterans in the form of the GI Bill of 1944.

No matter the outcome of the Poor People's Campaign, King insisted, he would win a moral victory. As he told a union rally in New York City on March 10, 1968, "People ask me, 'Suppose you go to Washington and you don't get anything? You ask people and you mobilize and you organize, and you don't get anything. You've been an absolute failure.' My only answer is that when you stand up for justice, you can never fail."[21]

King's aggressive new posture was exposing him to another risk besides failure. He was issuing an ultimatum: either Washington politicians approve the revolutionary ideology he advocated or his army of poor people would paralyze the business of Washington. He would be more visible and controversial than ever. His tactics were sure to provoke a harsh backlash.

The establishment would vilify him, and he knew it. King was putting his life in greater jeopardy, and he knew that too.

At Ebenezer Church on February 4, he preached his own eulogy in what became known as the Drum Major Sermon.[22] If his congregants read between the lines, they understood that he was sermonizing about his imminent death and how he had come to terms with it. He began by quoting from the tenth chapter of the Gospel of Mark. It tells of two apostles of Jesus—James and John—seeking to sit beside him in glory. In King's telling, Jesus responds that "whosoever will be great among you" shall be thy servant, and "whosoever will be the chiefest shall be the servant of all."

From that homage to humble service to others, as exemplified by Jesus, King drew a moral for himself. He went on to reflect on his low regard for what he called the "drum major instinct." He conceded, "We all want to be important, to surpass others, to achieve distinction, to lead the parade." He noted how that instinct can lead people astray in many ways—extravagant spending on cars and houses, self-puffery, crime, false gossip, a racist sense of superiority, and other evils.

Then he turned to his own legacy. That thought had him ruminating about his death, his funeral, and the kind of eulogy he would want. His legacy, he said, he would leave to the Ebenezer congregation to define. Not entirely, though. He implored them to remember him not for his Nobel Peace Prize or his three or four hundred other awards.

No, he cried out, as the sermon reached its climax, if they should remember him as a drum major, he beseeched them to remember him as a drum major for justice and righteousness. His voice taut, he went on to say that if he could do his Christian duty and "bring salvation to a world once wrought, if I can spread the message as the master taught," then his life would not have been in vain.[23]

He imagined that he would die with a sense of redemptive virtue. That was the compensation he sought.

– Epilogue –

Eluding a massive manhunt to capture him, JAMES EARL RAY remained at large for sixty-five days after King's death. On June 8, as he attempted to leave Heathrow Airport in London, bound for Brussels, he was identified and arrested. To avoid a jury trial that might have resulted in his execution, on March 10, 1969, he pleaded guilty in a Memphis courtroom to first-degree murder and was sentenced to ninety-nine years in prison. Three days later, he denied having shot King, claiming that he was the dupe of a conspiracy. Despite intensive investigations by the FBI, a Justice Department task force, and the House Select Committee on Assassinations, no specific conspiracy was established, though the congressional committee theorized, based on circumstantial evidence, that some individuals, possibly one or both of Ray's brothers John and Jerry, might have been coconspirators with him. Ray died in a Nashville prison of kidney failure and complications from liver disease on April 23, 1998. He was seventy.

. . .

HENRY LOEB never wavered from his stand not to negotiate directly with the sanitation workers' union. Within two weeks of King's death, the Memphis city council reached a settlement with the union, providing a dues checkoff through the credit union, union recognition, and a ten-cent increase in hourly pay. Loeb did not officially ink the settlement but did not stand in the way of its adoption. He left the mayoralty when his term ended in 1972 and relocated to a farm near Forrest City, Arkansas. In 1988 he suffered a stroke that left him unable to speak. He died four years later at the age of seventy-one.

. . .

FRANK HOLLOMAN retired as Memphis police and fire director in 1970 to become security coordinator at the University of Missouri. In a speech to members of a security-industry association five months after King's death, he stated that the involvement of "outside people" had caused the trouble in Memphis that year by "inflaming the Negro community."[1]

. . .

LUCIUS BURCH practiced law in Memphis until shortly before his death in 1996 at eighty-four.

. . .

WILLIE RICHMOND served for thirty-two years as a police officer in Memphis. He became eligible to take the police department's test for promotion to lieutenant in 1973. He scored one hundred but was not promoted until 1979. He and one other policeman were the first two blacks to make lieutenant. Richmond retired from the force in 1997 as a captain.

. . .

JOE WARREN remained active in AFSCME Local 1733 for many years. He was one of eight former sanitation workers—participants in the strike of 1968—honored by President Obama in a White House ceremony in April 2011. Warren died of a heart attack in 2012. He was ninety-one.

. . .

GEORGIA DAVIS served as a Kentucky state senator for twenty-one years, championing legislation to end discrimination in employment and discrimination by sex and age. She married James Powers in 1973 and took his name. She was widely regarded as one of the most influential civil rights leaders in the history of Kentucky. She died of congestive heart failure on January 30, 2016, at the age of ninety-two.

. . .

ANDREW YOUNG served as congressman from Georgia's Fifth Congressional District, US ambassador to the United Nations, and mayor of Atlanta. Since retiring from politics in 1990, he has held positions with a variety of nonprofit organizations, including a term as president of the National Council of Churches.

. . .

JESSE JACKSON resigned as director of Operation Breadbasket in 1971 after a falling-out with Ralph Abernathy. He has continued to pursue civil rights and political causes as head of Rainbow/PUSH, based in Chicago. In 1984 and 1988 he unsuccessfully sought the Democratic nomination for president.

. . .

RALPH ABERNATHY succeeded King as president of the SCLC in April 1968. Along with Coretta King, he assumed leadership of the Poor People's Campaign, which commenced the next month. The antipoverty drive ended futilely after police, on June 24, drove hundreds of protesters from the shantytown they had erected near the Washington Memorial. When he refused to comply with orders to evacuate, Abernathy was jailed for nearly three weeks. He headed the SCLC for nine more years. He died of complications from blood clots on April 17, 1990, at the age of sixty-four.

. . .

After her husband's death, CORETTA KING played a prominent role as a political activist supporting the causes of African Americans, women, and gay people. In 1968 she founded the King Center for Nonviolent Social Change in Atlanta. She died of ovarian cancer on January 30, 2006. She was seventy-eight.

– Notes –

CHAPTER I: ATLANTA DEPARTURE

Ralph David Abernathy, *And the Walls Came Tumbling Down: An Autobiography* (New York: Harper & Row, 1989), 419.

1. Coretta Scott King, *My Life with Martin Luther King, Jr.* (New York: Penguin Books, 1993), 290.

2. G. Wayne Dowdy, *A Brief History of Memphis* (Charleston, SC: History Press, 2011), 63.

3. Joan Turner Beifuss, *At the River I Stand: Memphis, the 1968 Strike, and Martin Luther King* (orig. pub., 1985; Memphis: St. Lukes Press, 1990), 256.

4. E. H. Arkin, *Civil Disorders, Memphis, Tennessee, Feb. 12–April 12, 1968*, report of Memphis Police Dept., 36–37, Frank Holloman Collection, Shelby County Room, Memphis Public Library, Memphis, Tennessee (hereafter Holloman Collection).

5. Michael K. Honey, *Going Down Jericho Road: The Memphis Strike, Martin Luther King's Last Campaign* (New York: W. W. Norton, 2007), 376.

6. Stephen B. Oates, *Let the Trumpet Sound: The Life of Martin Luther King, Jr.* (New York: Harper & Row, 1982), 238.

7. David L. Lewis, *King: A Critical Biography* (New York: Praeger, 1970), 383.

8. Ibid.

9. FBI memo from New York Bureau to headquarters, April 1, 1968, transcript of conversation between King and Stanley Levison, King FOIA file 00000172–176.TIF.

10. David Garrow, *Bearing the Cross: Martin Luther King, Jr. and the Southern Leadership Conference* (orig. pub., 1986; New York: Perennial Classics, 2004), 391; Abernathy, *And the Walls Came Tumbling Down*, 323; and Taylor Branch, *At Canaan's Edge: America in the King Years, 1965–68* (New York: Simon & Schuster, 2006), 513.

11. Gerold Frank, *An American Death: The True Story of the Assassination of Dr. Martin Luther King, Jr. and the Greatest Manhunt of Our Time* (New York: Doubleday, 1972), 91.

12. Harry Belafonte with Michael Shnayerson, *My Song: A Memoir* (New York: Knopf, 2011), 311.

13. Tavis Smiley, *Death of a King: The Real Story of Dr. Martin Luther King Jr.'s Final Year* (New York: Little, Brown, 2014), 74.

14. Michael Eric Dyson, *I May Not Get There with You: The True Martin Luther King, Jr.* (New York: Free Press, 2000), 6.

15. Ralph Abernathy, testimony, August 14, 1978, in *Report of the Select Committee on Assassinations of the US House of Representatives Ninety-Fifth Congress, Second Session* (Washington, DC: Government Printing Office, 1979) (hereafter cited as HSCA testimony), vol. 1, 18.

16. Dorothy F. Cotton, *If Your Back's Not Bent: The Role of the Citizenship Education Program in the Civil Rights Movement* (New York: Atria Books, 2012), 260.

17. Dorothy F. Cotton, author interview by telephone, February 18, 2013.

18. Andrew Young, author interview, Atlanta, October 12, 2012.

19. Abernathy, *And the Walls Came Tumbling Down*, 428.

CHAPTER 2: DETOUR

Martin Luther King Jr. at Stanford, "The Other America," 1967, available at YouTube, https://www.youtube.com/watch?v=m3H978KlR20.

1. Martin Luther King Jr., "Remaining Awake Through a Great Revolution," National Cathedral, Washington, DC, March 31, 1968, in *A Testament of Hope: The Essential Writings and Speeches of Martin Luther King Jr.*, ed. James M. Washington (New York: HarperOne, 1986), 272–73.

2. Ibid., 275.

3. Briefcase contents, Morehouse College: Martin Luther King Jr. Collection, Robert W. Woodruff Library, Atlanta University Center, Atlanta (hereafter cited as Woodruff Library).

4. Martin Luther King Jr., unpublished manuscript, October 14, 1966, 1–2, Woodruff Library.

5. Helen B. Shaffer, "Negroes in the North," in *Editorial Research Reports 1965*, vol. II, 779–97 (Washington, DC: CQ Press, 1965), http://library.cqpress.com /cqresearcher/cqresrre1965102700.

6. Martin Luther King Jr., *Where Do We Go from Here: Chaos or Community?* (orig. pub. 1964; Boston: Beacon Press, 2010), 21.

7. Ibid., 107.

8. Martin Luther King Jr., "Beyond Vietnam: A Time to Break Silence," speech delivered April 4, 1967, at Riverside Church, New York City, *Common Dreams*, http://www.commondreams.org/views04/0115–13.htm.

9. Martin Luther King Jr., "Need to Go to Washington," unpublished transcript of a news conference, Atlanta, January 16, 1968, 1–6, archives of King Center for Nonviolent Social Change, Atlanta (hereafter King Center archives).

10. Garrow, *Bearing the Cross*, 615.

11. King, "Remaining Awake," 272–73.

12. Martin Luther King Jr., transcript of a speech, Waycross, Georgia, March 22, 1968, 3–6, King Center archives.

13. King schedule, Southern Christian Leadership Conference Records, William Rutherford Files, box 197, folder 9, item 3810, Stuart A. Rose Manuscript, Archives, and Rare Book Library, Emory University, Atlanta.

14. Marion Logan interview by Paul Steckler, December 9, 1988, in *Eyes on the Prize II Interviews*, Blackside, Inc., Washington University Libraries, Film and Media Archive, Henry Hampton Collection, http://digital.wustl.edu/e/eii/eiiweb /log5427.0673.097marianlogan.html.

CHAPTER 3: THE STRIKE

1. Honey, *Going Down Jericho Road*, 143.

2. Oates, *Let the Trumpet Sound*, 457.

3. Taylor Rogers, author interview, Memphis, October 12, 2006.

4. Samuel "Billy" Kyles, author interview, Memphis, April 13, 2007.

5. Ibid.

6. Gene Dattel, *Cotton and Race in the Making of America: The Human Costs of Economic Power* (Lanham, MD: Ivan R. Dee, 2009), 331.

7. Joe Warren, author interview, Memphis, October 12, 2006.

8. Ibid.

9. Rogers interview.

10. Warren interview.

11. Ibid.

12. Martin Luther King Jr., "Speech to Sanitation Workers," transcript, Memphis, March 18, 1968, 2, King Center archives.

13. Honey, *Going Down Jericho Road*, 63.

14. T. O. Jones, interview transcripts, August 8, 1969 and January 30, 1970, folders 108–10, Sanitation Strike Archival Project, Special Collections Department, Ned R. McWherter Library, University of Memphis (hereafter SSAP).

15. Beifuss, *At the River I Stand*, 32.

16. Warren interview.

17. Ibid.

18. Beifuss, *At the River I Stand*, 38.

19. Rogers interview.

20. Larry Scroggs, "New Union Command Post Hints 'We're Here to Stay,'" *Commercial Appeal*, March 18, 1968.

21. Beifuss, *At the River I Stand*, 375.

CHAPTER 4: AIRPORT ARRIVAL

Hampton Sides, *Hellhound on His Trail: The Stalking of Martin Luther King Jr. and the International Hunt for His Assassin* (New York: Doubleday, 2010), 122.

1. Beifuss, *At the River I Stand*, 375.

2. "Re: Security and Surveillance of Dr. Martin Luther King Jr.," Memphis police report by Inspector G. P. Tines, July 17, 1968, 2, Holloman Collection (hereafter Tines report).

3. James Lawson, author interview, Nashville, April 16, 2007.

4. Tines report, 4.

5. "King Challenges Court Restraint, Vows to March," *Commercial Appeal*, April 4, 1968.

6. Abernathy, *And the Walls Came Tumbling Down*, 12.

7. Author's recollection of comments heard while riding in a squad car during the summer of 1968.

8. Flip Schulke and Penelope O. McPhee, *King Remembered* (orig. pub., 1986; New York: W. W. Norton, 1989), 240–41.

9. Edward Estes Redditt, author interview, Somerville, Tennessee, October 12, 2006.

CHAPTER 5: THE INVITATION

Martin Luther King Jr., "Remaining Awake Through a Great Revolution," National Cathedral, Washington, DC, March 31, 1968, http://kingencyclopedia .stanford.edu/encyclopedia/documentsentry/doc_remaining_awake_through _a_great_revolution.1.html.

1. Samuel S. B. (Billy) Kyles, interview transcript, July 30, 1968, tape 280, 10, SSAP.

2. Kyles interview.

3. Rev. James M. Lawson Jr., interview transcript, July 8, 1970, tape 243, 8, SSAP.

4. Young interview.

5. Andrew Young, *An Easy Burden: The Civil Rights Movement and the Transformation of America* (New York: HarperCollins, 1996), 190.

6. Ibid.

7. Garrow, *Bearing the Cross*, 464.

8. Benjamin Hooks, author interview, Memphis, October 11, 2007.

9. "Young Criticizes Dr. King for Viet Statement," *Washington Post*, September 12, 1965.

10. Young, *Easy Burden*, 434.

11. Cotton, *If Your Back's Not Bent*, 209.

12. Young interview.

13. Ibid.

14. Ibid.

15. Honey, *Going Down Jericho Road*, 296.

16. Beifuss, *At the River I Stand*, 256.

17. Kyles interview, SSAP, 18–19.

18. King, "Speech to Sanitation Workers," 7.

19. Beifuss, *At the River I Stand*, 259.

CHAPTER 6: THE MAYOR

Martin Luther King Jr., "Memphis Sanitation Workers Strike," *King Encyclopedia*, http://kingencyclopedia.stanford.edu/encyclopedia/encyclopedia/enc_memphis_sanitation_workers_strike_1968/.

1. Young interview.

2. Lewis R. Donelson III, *Lewie* (Memphis: Rhodes College, 2012), 166–67.

3. Dowdy, *A Brief History of Memphis*, 27.

4. Frank L. McRae, author interview, Memphis, October 11, 2006.

5. Joseph Sweat, author interview, Nashville, April 16, 2007.

6. Beifuss, *At the River I Stand*, 62.

7. Quoting an ad from the *Memphis Appeal*, December 2, 1846, in Paul R. Coppock, *Memphis Memoirs* (Memphis: Memphis State University Press, 1980), 98.

8. Ibid., 73–74.

9. Sweat interview.

10. Beifuss, *At the River I Stand*, 206.

11. McRae interview.

12. King, "Speech to Sanitation Workers," 4.

13. McRae interview.

14. Martin Luther King Jr., *Why We Can't Wait* (orig. pub. 1963; New York: Signet Classic, 2000), 122.

15. Sweat interview.

16. Lewis R. Donelson, author interview, Memphis, April 4, 2014.

17. Quoted in Frank Murtaugh and Marilyn Sadler, "The Lions in Winter: Ten Civil Rights Pioneers Take Us Back to the Dark Days of April 1968," *Memphis*, April 8, 2008, 65.

18. Sweat interview.

19. Honey, *Going Down Jericho Road*, 20.

20. Ibid., 71.

21. Henry Loeb, interview transcript, tape 18, SSAP, 19.

CHAPTER 7: LORRAINE CHECK-IN

Sides, *Hellhound on His Trail*, 123.

1. W. P. Huston, "Supplemental Report on James Earl Ray," August 22, 1968, 2, Criminal Investigation Division, Memphis Police Department.

2. Beifuss, *At the River I Stand*, 355.

3. Abernathy, HSCA testimony, vol. 1, 32.

4. Beifuss, *At the River I Stand*, 356.

5. Abernathy, HSCA testimony, vol. 1, 32.

6. Honey, *Going Down Jericho Road*, 365.

7. Charles Cabbage, quoted in *Southern Patriot* (Southern Conference Educational Fund) article by Robert Analvage, as reported by the Memphis FBI bureau, April 5, 1968, Ernest Withers, FOIA file, 13.

8. Cotton interview.

9. Young interview.

10. Cotton, *If Your Back's Not Bent*, xiv.

11. Adam Fairclough, *To Redeem the Soul of America: The Southern Christian Leadership Conference and Martin Luther King, Jr.* (Athens: University of Georgia Press, 1987), 169.

12. Branch, *At Canaan's Edge*, 742.

13. Honey, *Going Down Jericho Road*, 379.

14. Branch, *At Canaan's Edge*, 742.

15. Oates, *Let the Trumpet Sound*, 281–82.

16. Branch, *At Canaan's Edge*, 742.

17. Cotton interview.

18. King, *My Life with Martin Luther King*, 289.

19. Marshall Frady, *Jesse: The Life and Pilgrimage of Jesse Jackson* (New York: Simon & Schuster, 2006), 226.

CHAPTER 8: DAMAGE CONTROL

Transcript of interview with James M. Lawson Jr., July 8, 1970, tape 243, SSAP, 7.

1. David Caywood, author interview, Memphis, April 7, 2014.

2. Frank Holloman, May 23, 1978, HSCA testimony, vol. 1, 258.

3. Donald Smith, May 23, 1978, HSCA testimony, vol. 1, 259–61.

4. Beifuss, *At the River I Stand*, 354.

5. Memo from Memphis FBI office, April 6, 1968, "Sanitation Workers Strike, Memphis, Tennessee, Racial Matters," 7–8.

6. Jesse Jackson, *Commercial Appeal*, video posted on its website, April 1, 2008.

7. Order of Judge Bailey Brown, City of Memphis v. Martin Luther King Jr. et al., April 3, 1968, US District Court, Western District of Tennessee, Western Division, Memphis.

8. Martin Luther King Jr., "I See the Promised Land, April 3, 1968," in Washington, *Testament of Hope*, 282.

9. Lawson interview.

10. McRae interview.

11. Lawson interview.

12. Young interview.

13. Abernathy, *And the Walls Came Tumbling Down*, 219.

14. Hooks interview.

15. Lawson interview.

CHAPTER 9: THE INJUNCTION

Oates, *Let the Trumpet Sound*, 191.

1. Tines report, 2.

2. Hearing transcript, City of Memphis v. Martin Luther King Jr. et al., April 4, 1968, US District Court, Western District of Tennessee, Western Division, Memphis, 203.

3. J. Michael Cody, author interview, Memphis, October 7, 2009.

4. Lucius E. Burch Jr. (1912–1996), *The Tennessee Encyclopedia of History and Culture*, Version 2.0, http://tennesseeencyclopedia.net/.

5. Caywood interview.

6. Cody interview.

7. Ibid.

8. Beifuss, *At the River I Stand*, 352.

9. Lucius Burch, interview transcript, September 3, 1968, tape 88, SSAP, 3.

10. Beifuss, *At the River I Stand*, 356.

11. Burch interview, 7, SSAP.

12. J. Michael Cody, quoted in "The Lions in Winter," 58.

13. Beifuss, *At the River I Stand*, 357.

14. Martin Luther King Jr., "Letter from Birmingham City Jail," in Washington, *Testament of Hope*, 293.

15. Burch interview, SSAP, 7.

16. Caywood interview.

17. Cody interview.

18. Ibid.

CHAPTER 10: INVADERS

1. Oates, *Let the Trumpet Sound*, 382.

2. Martin Luther King Jr., *In a Single Garment of Destiny: A Global Vision of Justice*, ed. Lewis V. Baldwin (Boston: Beacon Press, 2012), 128–29.

3. Martin Luther King Jr., "Need to Go to Washington," 9.

4. Beifuss, *At the River I Stand*, 334.

5. Cotton, *If Your Back's Not Bent*, 204.

6. Coby Smith, author interview, Memphis, October 8, 2007.

7. Quoted in "As American as Apple Pie, Cherry Pie—and Violence," *This Day in Quotes*, July 27, 2015, http://www.thisdayinquotes.com/2013/07/as-american -as-apple-pie-cherry-pie-and.html.

8. Appendix to field report from Memphis FBI office, "Black Organizing Project," Invaders FOIA file, 1.

9. Honey, *Going Down Jericho Road*, 235.

10. "Re: Sanitation Workers Strike, March 29, 1968," field report from Memphis FBI office, Exhibit F-456, in HSCA, vol. 1, 475.

11. FBI field report from Memphis office, February 27, 1968, Ernest Withers FOIA file, WP13, 4–5.

12. David J. Garrow, *The FBI and Martin Luther King, Jr.: From "Solo" to Memphis* (New York: W. W. Norton, 1981), 191.

13. Memo from Memphis FBI office, April 3, 1968, "Sanitation Workers Strike, Memphis, Tennessee, Racial Matters."

14. Donzaleigh Abernathy, *Partners to History: Martin Luther King Jr., Ralph David Abernathy and the Civil Rights Movement* (New York: Crown Publishers, 2003), 184.

15. Fairclough, *To Redeem the Soul of America*, 289.

16. John Burl Smith, HSCA testimony, November 20, 1978, vol. 6, 489.

17. Charles Cabbage, HSCA testimony, November 20, 1978, vol. 6, 516.

18. Fairclough, *To Redeem the Soul of America*, 380.

19. Marrell McCollough, HSCA testimony, vol. 6, 417.

20. Field report from Memphis FBI, April 6, 1968, Ernest Withers FOIA file, WP 14, 8–9.

21. Cabbage, HSCA testimony, 518.

22. John Burl Smith, HSCA testimony, November 20, 1978, vol. 6, 465–66.

23. Honey, *Going Down Jericho Road*, 414.

24. Charles Cabbage, HSCA testimony, November 20, 1978, vol. 6, 518.

CHAPTER 11: NINE-TO-FIVE SECURITY

Garrow, *Bearing the Cross*, 607

1. John Lewis with Michael D'Orso, *Walking with the Wind: A Memoir of the Movement* (New York: Simon & Schuster, 1998), 404.

2. Frank C. Holloman affidavit, filed April 3, 1968, City of Memphis v. Martin Luther King Jr. et al., US District Court, Western District of Tennessee, Western Division, 4.

3. Frank Holloman, testimony April 3, 1968, hearing transcript, City of Memphis v. Martin Luther King Jr. et al., US District Court, Western District of Tennessee, Western Division, 9.

4. Holloman, HSCA testimony, vol. 1, 253.

5. Tines report.

6. Young interview.

7. King, *My Life with Martin Luther King*, 226.

8. Young interview.

9. Beifuss, *At the River I Stand*, 353.

10. Holloman testimony, *City of Memphis v. Martin Luther King Jr. et al.*, 55.

11. Donald Smith, HSCA testimony in executive session, March 1978, vol. 4, Exhibit F-188, 259–61.

12. Tines report, 4.

13. Holloman, HSCA testimony, vol. 1, 263.

14. Ibid.

15. Frank Holloman, interview transcript, May 9, 1973, tape 355, SSAP, 8.

16. Oates, *Let the Trumpet Sound*, 191.

17. FBI memo from Las Vegas Bureau, May 15, 1964, Martin Luther King Jr. FOIA file, 00000224–5.TIF.

18. Branch, *At Canaan's Edge*, 10–11.

19. Frank, *American Death*, 89.

20. Gerald Posner, *Killing the Dream: James Earl Ray and the Assassination of Martin Luther King, Jr.* (New York: Random House, 1998), 5.

21. Maxine Smith, author interview, Memphis, October 12, 2007.

22. Caywood interview.

23. Gregory Jaynes, e-mail to the author, December 8, 2006.

24. Lawson interview.

25. Jerry Dave Williams, testimony in *Coretta Scott King et al. v. Loyd Jowers*, November 17, 1999, 315, Circuit Court of Shelby County, Thirtieth Judicial District, Memphis.

26. Redditt interview.

27. Ibid.

CHAPTER 12: RELUCTANT SPEAKER

King, *Where Do We Go from Here.*

1. Abernathy, *And the Walls Came Tumbling Down*, 430.

2. Garrow, *Bearing the Cross*, 354.

3. Branch, *At Canaan's Edge*, 513.

4. Frank, *An American Death*, 90.

5. Young interview.

6. Young, *Easy Burden*, 461; Richard Lischer, *The Preacher King: Martin Luther King, Jr. and the Word That Moved America* (Oxford, UK: Oxford University Press, 1995), 134.

7. Beifuss, *At the River I Stand*, 277.

8. Frady, *Jesse*, 224.

9. Branch, *At Canaan's Edge*, 216.

10. Young interview.

11. Branch, *At Canaan's Edge*, 184.

12. Lischer, *Preacher King*, 163.

13. Andrew Young, panel discussion, "Scoop: The Evolution of a Southern Reporter," January 16, 2013, Carter Library and Museum, Atlanta.

14. Frady, *Jesse*, 224.

15. Ibid., 226.

16. Abernathy, *And the Walls Came Tumbling Down*, 430.

17. Candadai Seshachari, "The Re-Making of a Leader: Martin Luther King's Last Phase," *Weber: The Contemporary West* 10, no. 2 (Spring/Summer 1993).

18. Frank, *American Death*, 39.

19. Ibid., 40–41.

20. Logan interview, 4.

21. Ibid., 1.

22. Ibid., 3–4.

23. SCLC Charter, appendix to FBI memo from J. F. Blandi to W. C. Sullivan, January 4, 1962, Sec. 6, Martin Luther King Jr. FOIA file, 4.

24. King, "I See the Promised Land," 5.

25. Clayborne Carson, *Martin's Dream: My Journey and the Legacy of Martin Luther King, Jr.: A Memoir* (New York: Palgrave Macmillan, 2013).

26. King, *Where Do We Go from Here*, 141.

27. Ibid., 173.

28. Martin Luther King Jr., "Showdown for Non-Violence," *Look*, April 16, 1968, 24–26.

29. Logan interview, 6.

30. FBI memo from G. C. Moore to William Sullivan, March 11, 1968, citing a report, *Martin Luther King, Jr.—A Current Analysis*, Martin Luther King Jr. FOIA file.

31. Frank, *American Death*, 39–40.

32. Garrow, *Bearing the Cross*, 591–92.

33. Belafonte, *My Song*, 328.

34. Martin Luther King Jr., "The Power of Nonviolence," speech at the University of California at Berkeley, July 4, 1957, *Journal of Christian Encounter/Intercollegian* 75, no. 8 (1957), 8–9, in Woodruff Library.

CHAPTER 13: THE STALKER

King, *Why We Can't Wait*.

1. Sides, *Hellhound on His Trail*, 305.

2. Frank, *An American Death*, 175.

3. William Bradford Huie, *He Slew the Dreamer: My Search for the Truth About James Earl Ray and the Murder of Martin Luther King* (Montgomery, AL: Black Belt Press, 1997), 26.

4. Ibid.

5. James Earl Ray, HSCA staff interview, Brushy Mountain State Penitentiary, Petros, Tennessee, March 22, 1977, HSCA, vol. 9, 17.

6. Posner, *Killing the Dream*, 85–86.

7. Frank, *An American Death*, 176.

8. Memo from Springfield, Illinois, FBI office to J. Edgar Hoover, August 1, 1969, HSCA Exhibit F-622, vol. 7, 422.

9. Posner, *Killing the Dream*, 108.

10. Ibid., 78.

11. Ibid., 102.

12. Ibid., 90–94.

13. George McMillan, *The Making of an Assassin: The Life of James Earl Ray* (Boston: Little, Brown, 1976), 111–12.

14. Posner, *Killing the Dream*, 98–100.

15. Ibid., 104–5.

16. Percy Foreman, testimony, April 4, 1974, HSCA, vol. 5, 335.

17. Posner, *Killing the Dream*, 109–10.

18. Ibid., 123–24.

19. Robert Blakey statement, November 10, 1978, HSCA, vol. 4, 195.

20. McMillan, *Making of an Assassin*, 228–29.

21. James Earl Ray testimony, March 28, 1977, HSCA, vol. 9, 262–63.

22. Summary of prosecutor's opening argument, *State of Tennessee v. James Earl Ray*, Criminal Court of Shelby County, Tennessee, 3/10/69, National Civil Rights Museum, Memphis, 4.

23. Staff report, HSCA, based on interview with Manuela Aguirre Medrano, November 1, 1978, HSCA, vol. 4, 158–59.

24. Ibid., 111–13.

25. Staff report, HSCA, November 10, 1978, vol. 4, 112–24, 158–59.

26. Percy Foreman testimony, HSCA, vol. 5, 95.

27. Staff report, HSCA, vol. 4, 122.

28. Evidence summary by US Representative Walter Fauntroy, November 9, 1978, HSCA, vol. 4, 5–6.

29. Huie, *He Slew the Dreamer*, 136.

30. Honey, *Going Down Jericho Road*, 408.

31. Huie, *He Slew the Dreamer*, 138.

32. Honey, *Going Down Jericho Road*, 408.

CHAPTER 14: SUMMONING DR. KING

Martin Luther King Jr., *"All Labor Has Dignity,"* ed. Michael K. Honey (Boston: Beacon Press, 2011).

1. Cody interview.

2. James Lawson, interview transcript, July 8, 1970, tape 244, series X, 60, SSAP; Tines report, 42.

3. Warren interview.

4. Rogers interview.

5. Beifuss, *At the River I Stand*, 362.

6. Abernathy, *Partners to History*, 147.

7. Honey, *Going Down Jericho Road*, 47.

8. Ibid., 185.

9. Ibid., 47.

10. Martin Luther King Jr., *Stride Toward Freedom: The Montgomery Story* (New York: Ballantine, 1958), 204.

11. King, *Where Do We Go from Here*, 149.

12. Edward E. Redditt, field report, to Memphis Police Dept., April 4, 1968, Exhibit F-299, HSCA, vol. 4, 205–7.

13. Arkin, *Civil Disorders*, 42.

14. Honey, *Going Down Jericho Road*, 359–60.

15. Ibid., 358.

16. Interview by the *Commercial Appeal*, posted online April 1, 2008.

17. Ibid., 431.

18. Abernathy, *And the Walls Came Tumbling Down*, 430–31.

19. Beifuss, *At the River I Stand*, 363.

20. Abernathy, *And the Walls Came Tumbling Down*, 432.

21. King, "I See the Promised Land," 279.

22. Lewis, *King*, 51.

23. Belafonte, *My Song*, 247.

24. Andrew Young and Kabir Sehgal, *Walk in My Shoes: Conversations Between a Civil Rights Legend and His Godson on the Journey Ahead* (New York: Palgrave Macmillan, 2010), 154.

25. Taylor Branch, *Pillar of Fire: America in the King Years, 1963–65* (New York: Touchstone, 1998), 541.

26. Abernathy, *And the Walls Came Tumbling Down*, 432.

27. Clayborne Carson, e-mail to author, May 17, 2015.

28. Abernathy, *And the Walls Came Tumbling Down*, 433.

29. Honey, *Going Down Jericho Road*, 417.

CHAPTER 15: FROM THE MOUNTAINTOP

"Palm Sunday Sermon on Mohandas K. Gandhi, Delivered at Dexter Avenue Baptist Church," March 22, 1959, Martin Luther King, Jr. Papers Project, Stanford University, https://swap.stanford.edu/20141218225655/http://mlk-kpp01.stanford.edu/primarydocuments/Vol5/22Mar1959_PalmSundaySermononMohandasK.Gandhi,DeliveredAtDext.pdf.

1. Beifuss, *At the River I Stand*, 364.

2. King, "I See the Promised Land," 279.

3. Kyles interview.

4. King, *Stride Toward Freedom*, 59.

5. King, "I See the Promised Land," 279.

6. Martin Luther King Jr., "Our God Is Marching On," Montgomery, Alabama, March 25, 1965, in Washington, *Testament of Hope*, 227.

7. Lischer, *Preacher King*, 232.

8. King, *Parting the Waters*, 65–66.

9. Notebook of Martin Luther King Jr., Martin Luther King, Jr., Collection, Woodruff Library.

10. King, "I See the Promised Land," 286.

11. Schulke and McPhee, *King Remembered*, 59–60.

12. Frank, *An American Death*, 89.

13. Martin Luther King Jr., "The Drum Major Instinct," February 4, 1968, in Washington, *Testament of Hope*, 266–67.

14. King, *My Life with Martin Luther King*, 284.

15. Honey, *Going Down Jericho Road*, 452.

16. King, *My Life with Martin Luther King*, 292.

17. Cody interview.

18. Beifuss, *At the River I Stand*, 368.

19. "Power, Prescience of King's 'Mountaintop' Speech," *Weekend Edition*, National Public Radio, January 14, 2007, http://www.npr.org/templates/story/story.php?storyId=6854154.

20. Abernathy, *And the Walls Came Tumbling Down*, 433.
21. Frady, *Jesse*, 226.
22. Jackson, *Commercial Appeal* video.
23. Kyles interview.
24. Beifuss, *At the River I Stand*, 368.

CHAPTER 16: LONG NIGHT

Georgia Davis Powers, *I Shared the Dream: The Pride, Passion and Politics of the First Black Woman Senator from Kentucky* (Far Hills, NJ: New Horizon Press, 1995), 225–27, 173.

1. Honey, *Going Down Jericho Road*, 427.
2. Abernathy, *And the Walls Came Tumbling Down*, 434.
3. Ibid.
4. Report of the Department of Justice Task Force to Review the FBI Martin Luther King, Jr., Security and Assassinations Investigations, January 11, 1997, 29, National Archives, Washington, DC.
5. Georgia Davis Powers, author interview, Louisville, March 15, 2013.
6. Powers, *I Shared the Dream*, 222.
7. Ibid., 221.
8. Edward T. Brethitt, interview transcript by Betsy Brinson, February 24, 2000, Civil Rights Movement in Kentucky Oral History Project, Kentucky Historical Society, Lexington.
9. Powers interview.
10. Powers, *I Shared the Dream*, 85.
11. Ibid., 96.
12. Powers, *I Shared the Dream*, 100.
13. Ibid., 146.
14. Ibid., 172.
15. Ibid., 180.
16. Powers interview.
17. Powers, *I Shared the Dream*, 145–46.
18. Powers interview.
19. Powers, *I Shared the Dream*, 136.
20. Ibid., 162.
21. Powers interview.
22. Ibid.
23. Garrow, *Bearing the Cross*, 621.
24. Powers interview.
25. Powers, *I Shared the Dream*, 225–27.

CHAPTER 17: HOME PRESSURES

1. Marc Perrusquia, "Martin Luther King Jr.'s Last 32 Hours," *Commercial Appeal*, April 4, 2013.

2. King, *My Life with Martin Luther King*, 290.

3. Abernathy, *Partners to History*, 193.

4. King, *My Life with Martin Luther King*, 58.

5. Coretta Scott King as told to Rev. Dr. Barbara Reynolds, *My Life, My Love, My Legacy* (New York: Henry Holt, 2017), 166.

6. Carson, *Martin's Dream*, 191.

7. King, *My Life, My Love, My Legacy*, 7–10.

8. King, *My Life with Martin Luther King*, 24.

9. Carson, *Martin's Dream*, 182.

10. Garrow, *Bearing the Cross*, 38.

11. Branch, *At Canaan's Edge*, 677.

12. Fairclough, *To Redeem the Soul of America*, 391.

13. King, *My Life, My Love, My Legacy*, 97.

14. King, *My Life with Martin Luther King*, 142.

15. Dyson, *I May Not Get There with You*, 298.

16. Cotton, *If Your Back's Not Bent*, 94–95.

17. Cheryl Lynn Greenberg, "SNCC: Born of the Sit-Ins, Dedicated to Action: Remembrances of Mary Elizabeth King," from Trinity College SNCC Reunion, April 1988, Civil Rights Movement Veterans, http://www.crmvet.org /nars/maryking.htm, originally published in *A Circle of Trust: Remembering SNCC*, ed. Cheryl Lynn Greenberg (New Brunswick, NJ: Rutgers University Press, 1998).

18. Branch, *Pillar of Fire*, 325.

19. Garrow, *Bearing the Cross*, 375.

20. Oates, *Let the Trumpet Sound*, 158–59.

21. Branch, *Pillar of Fire*, 339.

22. King, *My Life with Martin Luther King*, 204.

23. Memo from the New York FBI Bureau, BU 100–442529, October 16, 1964, Martin Luther King Jr. FBI FOIA file.

24. Abernathy, *And the Walls Came Tumbling Down*, 471.

25. Branch, *At Canaan's Edge*, 678, 744; Garrow, *Bearing the Cross*, 617.

26. King, *My Life with Martin Luther King*, 55.

27. Abernathy, *And the Walls Came Tumbling Down*, 472–73.

28. Garrow, *Bearing the Cross*, 374.

29. Ibid., 96.

30. Garrow, *The FBI and Martin Luther King, Jr*, 125–26.

31. Young interview.

32. King, *My Life, My Love, My Legacy*, 259.

33. Abernathy, *And the Walls Came Tumbling Down*, 471.

34. Martin Luther King Jr., from sermon "Unfulfilled Dreams," March 3, 1968, quoted in Dyson, *I May Not Get There with You*, 162.

35. Garrow, *Bearing the Cross*, 617.

CHAPTER 18: INVADERS' EXIT

"Why We Must Go to Washington," transcript of King's remarks at SCLC retreat, January 16, 1968, Ebenezer Baptist Church, Atlanta, 10, King Center archives.

1. Garrow, *Bearing the Cross*, 622.

2. Honey, *Going Down Jericho Road*, 428.

3. Cotton, *If Your Back's Not Bent*, 263.

4. Perrusquia, "Martin Luther King Jr.'s Last 32 Hours."

5. Cotton, *If Your Back's Not Bent*, 264.

6. Hearing transcript, *City of Memphis v. Martin Luther King Jr. et al.*, April 3, 1968, US District Court, Western District of Tennessee, Western Division, 59–61.

7. Young interview.

8. Honey, *Going Down Jericho Road*, 428

9. Hooks interview.

10. Abernathy, *And the Walls Came Tumbling Down*, 437.

11. Fairclough, *To Redeem the Soul of America*, 381.

12. Ibid., 384.

13. Quoted in "As American as Apple Pie, Cherry Pie—and Violence."

14. Fairclough, *To Redeem the Soul of America*, 365–66.

15. Ibid., 359–60.

16. "Sanitation Workers Strike, Memphis, March 30, 1968," report from the Memphis FBI office to J. Edgar Hoover, MLK Exhibit 457, HSCA, vol. 6, 576.

17. James Lawson, interview transcript, July 8, 1970, tape 244, SSAP, 5.

18. Memo from Memphis FBI office, April 6, 1968, Ernest Withers FOIA File, 2.

19. FBI, Sanitation Workers Strike report, Exhibit 457, 573–76.

20. Marrell McCollough, November 20, 1978, HSCA testimony, vol. 6, 414–15.

21. Robert Blakey statement, November 20, 1978, HSCA testimony, vol. 6, 444.

22. Honey, *Going Down Jericho Road*, 432.

23. Memo from Memphis FBI office, April 6, 1968, Ernest Withers FOIA File, 8.

CHAPTER 19: MELANCHOLY AFTERNOON

Let the Trumpet Sound, 468.

1. Arkin, *Civil Disorders*, 43.

2. Abernathy, *And the Walls Came Tumbling Down*, 437–38.

3. Frank, *American Death*, 57.

4. King, *My Life with Martin Luther King*, 292.

5. Powers interview.

6. King, *My Life, My Love, My Legacy*, 5.

7. Branch, *Parting the Waters*, 40.

8. King, *My Life with Martin Luther King*, 76.

9. Branch, *At Canaan's Edge*, 761.

10. Powers interview.

11. Martin Luther King Jr., *"All Labor Has Dignity,"* ed. Michael K. Honey (Boston: Beacon Press, 2011), xxxiii.

12. Logan interview.

13. King, "Showdown for Non-Violence," 25.

14. Memo from Hosea Williams to Bernard Lafayette, February 11, 1968, item 3837, folder 1, box 198, William Rutherford Files, Southern Christian Leadership Conference Records, Stuart A. Rose Manuscript, Archives, and Rare Book Library, Robert W. Woodruff Library, Emory University (hereafter Rutherford Files).

15. Andrew Young, *A Way Out of No Way: The Spiritual Memoirs of Andrew W. Young* (Nashville: Thomas Nelson, 1994), 100.

16. "SCLC finances," FBI memo from Sullivan to Moore, October 28, 1967, Martin Luther King Jr. FOIA file, 00000119.TIF.

17. Honey, *Going Down Jericho Road*, 189.

18. King, *"All Labor Has Dignity,"* 153.

19. Memo from New York FBI office to Director, July 1, 1966, presumably based on wiretap of Stanley Levison, Martin Luther King Jr. FOIA file, 100–149194.TIF; memo from New York FBI office, September 21, 1966, quoting *New York Times*, Martin Luther King Jr. FOIA file, 00000063.TIF.

20. Letter from William Rutherford to Marlon Brando, February 28, 1968, item 3959, box 198, folder 14, Rutherford files.

21. Abernathy testimony, August 14, 1978, HSCA, vol. 1, 28–29.

22. "Re SCLC finances," February 29, 1968, FBI memo from Moore to Sullivan, Martin Luther King Jr. FOIA File, 00000180.TIF.

23. Fairclough, *To Redeem the Soul of America*, 369.

24. "Re: SCLC Finances and Poor People's Campaign," FBI memo, March 26, 1968, Martin Luther King Jr. FOIA file, 00000131–132.TIF.

25. "Why We Must Go to Washington," transcript of King's remarks at SCLC retreat, January 16, 1968, Ebenezer Baptist Church, Atlanta, 16, King Center archives.

26. Oates, *Let the Trumpet Sound*, 440.

27. King, "Showdown for Non-Violence," 24.

28. "Re Washington Spring Project," FBI memo from Moore to Jackson, Mississippi, office, March 11, 1968, HSCA, vol. 6, 27–29, 30.

29. Beifuss, *At the River I Stand*, 380.

30. Abernathy, *And the Walls Came Tumbling Down*, 438.

CHAPTER 20: RAY'S LUCKY BREAKS

King, *My Life with Martin Luther King*, 227.

1. James Earl Ray, interviewed by Dan Rather, CBS Special Reports, March 9, 1977, HSCA, vol. 1, 209.

2. Frank, *An American Death*, 59.

3. Report of the Select Committee on Assassinations of the US House of Representatives, JFK Assassination Records, Findings in the Assassination of Martin Luther King, Jr., National Archives, Washington, DC, 299.

4. McMillan, *Making of an Assassin*, 301.

5. Michael Finger, "31 Hours, 28 Minutes: A Timeline of Dr. Martin Luther King's Last Hours in Memphis," *Memphis*, April 2008, 53.

6. Opening statement by Shelby County district attorney Philip Canale, *State of Tennessee v. James Earl Ray*, Criminal Court of Shelby County, National Civil Rights Museum, Memphis, 2.

7. Charles Stephens's affidavit, exhibit in *Tennessee v. Ray*, 2, National Civil Rights Museum, Memphis.

8. Department of Justice task force report, National Civil Rights Museum, Memphis, 49.

9. Canale opening statement, National Civil Rights Museum, Memphis, 2.

CHAPTER 21: DARK NIGHT

Martin Luther King Jr., transcript of speech in Waycross, Georgia, 1.

1. Young interview.

2. Abernathy, *And the Walls Came Tumbling Down*, 440.

3. Jesse Jackson, interviewed online by Jeff McAdory, *Commercial Appeal*, April 4, 2013.

4. Frank, *An American Death*, 154.

5. Autopsy report by J. T. Francisco, M.D., Office of the Chief Medical Examiner, Tennessee Department of Public Health, Memphis, April 11, 1968, 1, http://www.autopsyfiles.org/reports/Celebs/king%20jr,%20martin%20luther_report.pdf.

6. Abernathy, *And the Walls Came Tumbling Down*, 440.

7. Young, *Easy Burden*, 464.

8. Beifuss, *At the River I Stand*, 383.

9. Abernathy, *And the Walls Came Tumbling Down*, 440–41.

10. Ibid., 442.

11. Attachment to findings in "United States Department of Justice Investigation of Recent Allegations Regarding the Assassination of Dr. Martin Luther King, Jr.," June 2000, regarding alleged involvement of Memphis police officers, Harold Weisberg Archive, http://jfk.hood.edu/Collection/Weisberg%20Subject%20Index%20Files/F%20Disk/FBI/FBI%20Office%20of%20Professional%20Responsibility%20Conclusions%20King/Item%202004.pdf, 37–42. See "List of Attachments," US Department of Justice, https://www.justice.gov/crt/list-attachments-0.

12. Young, *Easy Burden*, 465.

13. Jaynes note to author.

14. Young and Sehgal, *Walk in My Shoes*, 23.

15. King, *My Life with Martin Luther King*, 314.

CHAPTER 22: REDEMPTION

Paul Weeks, "Dr. King Under Heavy Guard on Arrival Here," *Los Angeles Times*, February 25, 1965.

1. Abernathy, HSCA testimony, vol. 1, 22.

2. Branch, *Parting the Waters*, 58–61.

3. Oates, *Let the Trumpet Sound*, 48.

4. Young, *Walk in My Shoes*, 23.

5. Maxine Smith interview.

6. Branch, *Parting the Waters*, 59–60.

7. Carson, *Martin's Dream*, 206.

8. King, *Stride Toward Freedom*, 94.

9. Ibid., 92.

10. Carson, *Martin's Dream*, 180.

11. Fairclough, *To Redeem the Soul of America*, 26.

12. King, *Stride Toward Freedom*, 34–35.

13. King, *My Life with Martin Luther King*, 151.

14. Martin Luther King Jr., "Suffering and Faith," *Christian Century*, 1960, 182–83.

15. Martin Luther King Jr., "Speech Accepting the Nobel Peace Prize," in Washington, *Testament of Hope*, 226.

16. Lischer, *Preacher King*, 192.

17. King, *Why We Can't Wait*, 128–29.

18. King, "Showdown for Non-Violence," 26.

19. Fairclough, *To Redeem the Soul of America*, 364.

20. Young interview.

21. Martin Luther King Jr., "Salute to Freedom," speech to Local 1199 of National Health Care Workers' Union, New York City, March 10, 1968, in *The Radical King*, ed. Cornel West (Boston: Beacon Press, 2015), 240.

22. King, "Drum Major Instinct," 259–67.

23. Washington, *Testament of Hope*, 267.

EPILOGUE

1. Frank C. Holloman, "Civil Disorders—Where To Now?," speech to the 14th Annual Seminar, American Society for Industrial Security, Fort Worth, Texas, September 11, 1968, Holloman Collection, 6.

– Acknowledgments –

MUCH OF THIS BOOK'S ORIGINALITY is owing to a series of interviews that I conducted with people who were close associates of Martin Luther King Jr. in March and April of 1968 or who were immersed in the events that brought him to Memphis at that time. I am indebted to them for having shared their recollections with me.

To document events that occurred five decades ago, I relied on extensive archival research. Particularly helpful in guiding me through the maze of relevant archives were Sara Cantrell of the National Civil Rights Museum, Ed Frank of the Ned R. McWherter Library at the University of Memphis, and Laurel Davis of the Boston College Law Library. I thank them, as well as Kira Jones, who researched the William Rutherford papers in the Stuart A. Rose Manuscript, Archives, and Rare Book Library at Emory University. I benefited, moreover, from access to records at the Memphis Public Library and Information Center, Shelby County Courthouse, Tennessee State Library and Archives, Federal Bureau of Investigation, Newton (Massachusetts) Free Library, and US National Archives and Records Administration.

I am beholden to the Atlanta University Center for having awarded me a travel grant to research the King Collection at its Robert W. Woodruff Library. I thank the Intellectual Properties Management, Inc., for permission to copy documents at the Woodruff Library. I am grateful to Ryan Jones, whose commentary during a tour of the National Civil Rights Museum deepened my understanding of what happened at the Lorraine Motel in April 1968. Vince Hughes, Ron Borod, and Wayne Dowdy kindly briefed me about events and context related to their city of Memphis. Friends Martha and Jerrold Graber shared their knowledge of Memphis and housed and fed me during several visits to the city. Philip and Ellen Rosenbloom graciously offered their hospitality in Louisville.

For legal help and insights into the publishing world, I was fortunate to have lawyers Rob Bertsche, Lloyd Constantine, and Bruce Kramer and book editor Barbara Grossman. For leads to literary agents or assistance with photos, I heartily thank Sarah and Josh Lamstein, Corby Kummer, Michael Useem, Lee Van Kirk, and Peter Cowen.

Colleagues and friends generously read early drafts and penned comments that helped shape the book. For that invaluable feedback at a critical stage in the book's gestation, I warmly thank Sue Bass, Mark Brodin, Frank Levy, David Whitford, Jim Wexler, and Seth and Alexa Rosenbloom. I owe a large debt of gratitude to the labor historian Michael Honey, who astutely critiqued a later draft.

My agent, William Clark, has been an indispensable ally at every stage of the publishing process. At Beacon Press, I have been blessed with a superb editor, Gayatri Patnaik. She enthusiastically embraced the book on a first reading and has nurtured it skillfully along ever since. I thank as well the rest of the top-notch team at Beacon, including Helene Atwan, Marcy Barnes, Susan Lumenello, Melissa Nasson, Nicholas DiSabatino, Pam MacColl, and Bob Kosturko.

I inflicted early versions of my manuscript on Paul Osterman and Evan Schouten. They brought their sharp eyes and sound judgment to the reading and assessing of it. They buoyed me throughout the whole editorial journey with unstinting support. I cannot thank them enough.

– Index –